FRANK WEDEKIND

*In Anerkennung
fuer gute Leistungen im
Studium der deutschen Sprache

überreicht vom
General Konsulat
der
Bundesrepublik Deutschland
in Detroit*

Caricature by Bruno Paul

MODERN GERMAN AUTHORS
New Series

EDITED BY R. W. LAST

VOLUME FOUR

FRANK WEDEKIND

by

ALAN BEST

*In Anerkennung
fuer gute Leistungen im
Studium der deutschen Sprache

überreicht vom
Generalkonsulat
der
Bundesrepublik Deutschland
in Detroit*

OSWALD WOLFF
London

Modern German Authors—New Series
ed. R. W. Last

Volume One: Heinrich Böll—Withdrawal and Re-emergence

Volume Two: Hermann Hesse—The Man who Sought and Found Himself

Volume Three: Erich Kästner

Volume Four: Frank Wedekind

isbn Cloth 0 85496 054 6
Paper 0 85496 055 4

© 1975 Oswald Wolff (Publishers) Limited
London W1M 6DR

printed in great britain by
clarke, doble & brendon ltd.,
plymouth

CONTENTS

	Preface	7
1	The Man Behind the Works	9
2	The Major Themes	22
3	The Three-Ring Circus	30
	(i) The Travelling Circus: *Fritz Schwigerling oder Der Liebestrank* (The Love-potion)	
	(ii) The Social Circus: *Der Kammersänger* (The Court Singer); *Die Zensur* (Censorship)	
	(iii) Escape from the Circus—Failure and Success: *Hidalla; Franziska*	
4	The Tragedy of Adolescence: *Frühlings Erwachen* (Spring Awakening)	64
5	The Rise and Fall of a Beautiful Dream: *Lulu*	82
6	Palaces and Kings—The Triumph of Bourgeois Society: *Der Marquis von Keith; König Nicolo* (King Nicolo)	98
	Conclusion	115
	Notes	117
	Select Bibliography	119

PREFACE

Wedekind's collected works[1] comprise some thirty plays and pantomimes, seventeen prose narratives, twenty-one essays on literary, cultural, social and political topics, nearly one hundred and fifty satirical, cabaret and political poems, and a collection of notes by the author on his plays. Only a fraction of this material is as yet available in English. The most comprehensive work on Wedekind is still the three volume critical biography by his contemporary Artur Kutscher,[2] which contains a detailed account of the contents of the works, their history, development and contemporary reaction. For the English reader the only full-length study of Wedekind to date is that by Sol Gittleman in the *Twayne World Author Series* (1969), which offers detailed accounts of the contents of nearly all the works in a general survey.

This present study has chosen a different approach. Deliberately selective in the material it discusses, its aim is to illustrate the characteristic themes and techniques of Wedekind's work. If it is successful the reader should gain a clearer understanding of the works discussed in detail, but also, and perhaps more importantly, should be able to approach other works by Wedekind with greater confidence and an awareness of the aims and preoccupations of the author. The study concentrates on Wedekind's drama and prefaces the works for which he is best known (*Spring Awakening, Earth Spirit, Pandora's Box, The Marquis of Keith* and *King Nicolo*—all of which have been translated into English) with a discussion of five lesser-known but representative plays, each of which highlights a particular aspect of Wedekind's approach with a clarity less immediately obvious in the more famous works. Wedekind writes to a fixed scenario, his plays lift the curtain on society from different angles, but whatever the setting and costume the intention is the same. Wedekind is a potent dramatic figure today because his critique of society stems from psychological conflicts in his characters which are as relevant now as they were in Wedekind's lifetime.

For permission to examine and quote from unpublished Wedekind material, acknowledgement and thanks are due to: Frau Kadidja Wedekind-Biel, Frau Pamela Wedekind-Regnier; Herr Richard Lemp, Director of the Manuscript Section of the Stadtbibliothek in Munich (Monacensia-Abteilung); the Kantonsbibliothek, Aarau, Switzerland.

I am indebted to the editors of *German Life and Letters* for permission to reproduce material originally published in my article 'The Censor Censored: An Approach to Frank Wedekind's *Die Zensur*' (1973).

The translations of the *Marquis of Keith* are from the text commissioned by the Royal Shakespeare Company for its 1974 London production, translated by Ronald Eyre and myself. All the other translations are mine.

1

THE MAN BEHIND THE WORKS

The events that accompanied Frank Wedekind's funeral in Munich on 12 March 1918 had a quality that could well have come from the writer's own pen. His young widow, distraught and on the verge of exhaustion, was accompanied behind the cortège by distinguished mourners from civic and artistic bodies and, so it seemed, half the bohemian life of the Bavarian capital, ably supported by a large contingent of ladies of the town. The latter, one eye-witness noted wryly, appeared out of a sense of collegiality. The cortège was preceded to the cemetery by a mad stampede in the hopes of obtaining a good vantage point, so that the official mourners were hopelessly cramped together and spent most of the ceremony treading on each other's toes and muttering imprecations at one another while jostling for a suitably dignified position.

This incongruous counterpoint to the reason for their presence was capped, however, by the activities of one Heinrich Lautensack, a young, precariously neurotic writer and admirer of Wedekind who had engaged a camera crew to film events for posterity; the mourners were constantly harangued as to how they should position themselves for the best effect as the camera crew climbed everywhere. When the coffin had been lowered into the ground, Lautensack, hysterical with grief, threw himself into the open grave, proclaiming his despair. Helped out, he returned to his rôle as director and continued to film the mourners as they dispersed.

Somehow it seems fitting that Wedekind, who had created such confusion and disorder about him while he lived, should provoke such a grotesque enactment of his last rites. Even in death he was denied the dignity that society had so diligently withheld during his lifetime. When he died his reputation amongst those of the public who had heard of him was for the most part that of a libertine, an anti-bourgeois exploiter of sexuality and a threat to public morality. This view was confirmed in many minds by the efforts of the small but vociferous group of writers and critics who made it their business to defend him. Only the creation of the Weimar Republic in Germany after World War One and the abolition of censorship cleared the way, and the 1920's saw a veritable surge of enthusiasm for Wedekind's work as the Expressionist generation and producers of Expressionist plays adopted and successfully restyled his works. For the first time, but not the last, the mood of an age caught up with Wedekind, and his reputation soared and spread to the United Kingdom and America. None the less his presentation of sexual problems and his portrayal of society made Wedekind anathema to many in Germany and the advent of National Socialism put an abrupt end to the Wedekind boom.

The Nazis did not quite know how to deal with him—they could hardly 'burn' him, for much of his vocabulary bore an unfortunate similarity to their own slogans. A writer who proposed an 'International League for the Propagation of Eugenic Health' in one of his plays could hardly be dismissed as decadent. They first tried to brand him as a Jew, and when this failed, brought pressure to bear on those who wished to sustain his reputation. Where the authorities were prepared to publish his work, as in a projected film version of *Der Marquis von Keith*, they required certain modifications. The Marquis is a shady character, a speculator, who makes his living by using other people's money to back his own grand schemes, and it was put to Wedekind's widow Tilly that Keith should be portrayed as a Jew. This she refused to allow and the film was never made. In the end the Nazis found a quiet but effective solution. The name of Wedekind was to disappear. His books were called in and pulped for newsprint, and performances or references to them were 'discouraged'.

The defeat of the Third Reich in 1945 allowed Wedekind to be introduced to a new generation, but like other pre-Nazi writers he was soon to be swamped in a deluge as thirteen years of western culture swept over Germany and demanded instant digestion. Too old to be truly modern and too recent to be a classic, Wedekind fell between two stools and suffered accordingly. However, by 1964, the centenary of his birth, he could be considered securely established and his reputation outside Germany was spreading beyond the specialist ranks of Germanists or devoted theatre students who had come to him via Eugene O'Neill or Bertolt Brecht. In particular *Lulu* and *Frühlings Erwachen* (Spring Awakening) have gone down well with Anglo-Saxon audiences and the recent productions of Peter Barnes's adaptation of *Lulu*[3] have cemented Wedekind's reputation as a 'safe' experimental writer for student and amateur production.

The sexual revolution that swept the United Kingdom in the 'sixties and bore away the function of the Lord Chamberlain as Censor for theatrical performance finally allowed Wedekind's works to be seen on their own merits as dramatic confrontations rather than sexual exhibitionism (provided, that is, directors can be restrained from undressing their leading actresses). No-one knew better than Wedekind the erotic mileage to be gained from black underwear, and he is on record as disapproving of an overtly sexual presentation of Lulu in 1917 by Maria Orska, whose costume was a transparent diaphanous veil and nothing else. His comment is not without relevance in our own 'liberated' age : 'Art is knowing what to leave out. She has put it all back again.'[4]

Wedekind began life an outsider and remained one. He was born in Hanover on 24 July 1864 to parents who had just returned from voluntary exile in the United States. (His father's liberal views had led to close involvement in the unsuccessful upheavals in Germany of 1848.) Wedekind's forenames, Benjamin Franklin, may serve as some indication of his father's enthusiasm for the land of the free. The New Germany of Bismarck and the Kaiser after 1871 hastened the family's departure to neutral and republican Switzerland where the sons were saved from the prospect of becoming Prussian cannon-fodder. In the confusions of these comings and goings Frank never acquired official German papers (as the child of American citizens he was automatically an American) and he was later to suffer considerable difficulties on this account.

The Wedekinds purchased Schloss Lenzburg in Canton Aargau to the south-east of Zurich and the sons went to school in the nearby Canton city of Aarau. Apart from some personal misdemeanours of varying gravity, Wedekind's scholastic career was unremarkable, and on leaving school he went first to Lausanne and then in 1884 to Munich, to study Law. He soon found literature more to his taste but omitted to so inform his father, who was paying the bills. When the deception was discovered there was a series of heated arguments culminating in a fearsome scene in the autumn of 1886 when both lost their tempers; Frank hit his father and stormed out of the house. He went to work in Zurich for the soup firm of Maggi where he lasted seven months as director of advertising, and then tried, unsuccessfully, to live from his journalistic writings. Eventually he was forced to write home suing for peace, his father relented and sent money to support him as a writer.

By now Wedekind was frequenting the Zurich literary scene, where amongst other authors he met the Hauptmann brothers; in one of his frequent low moods he confided the state and cause of his family situation to Gerhart Hauptmann, who, seeing its dramatic potential, stored the information away to use in his play *Das Friedensfest* (The Reconciliation, 1890). To those who knew the Wedekind family the parentage of the characters was immediately obvious. This breach of confidence kindled a feud that smouldered relentlessly until Wedekind's death and was in no way assuaged for Wedekind by the fact that Hauptmann enjoyed popular success while he did not. The numerous slighting references to Hauptmann in Wedekind's plays and the often libellous manuscript material still unpublished show Wedekind's ability to nurse a grudge.

Wedekind's father died suddenly in 1888 leaving his son the prospect of financial independence. There now followed years of travel and discovery. He visited and stayed in Berlin, Munich, Paris and London, meeting notable figures on the fringe of society and discovering and fostering in both Paris and Munich an enduring love for the circus. He frequented literary circles, enjoying the life of a Bohemian and the company of as many women as he could muster. Even so, financial circumstances began to make life difficult for him and his writing was not faring well. Though he was accepted by his colleagues, public recognition would not come and his inheritance was disappearing at an alarming rate. The publication of *Frühlings Erwachen* in 1891 and *Der Erdgeist* (The Earth Spirit) in 1895 revealed his talent but also his greatest problem. *Der Erdgeist*, the first version of the Lulu plays to be published, was a truncated version abridged at his publisher's insistence lest there be legal repercussions caused by the subject matter and manner of presentation.

The period after 1895 was a trying one for Wedekind: unable to persuade theatres to stage his work he earned a small amount writing for the Munich satirical magazine *Simplicissimus*. He found this soul-destroying and sought consolation in a relationship with Strindberg's former wife Frida Uhl. Their relationship was as mercurial as it was short-lived and was already on the wane when a son was born to them in August 1896.

Simplicissimus fought a running battle with the censor and especially with the Prussian authorities, so when a scathing satire on Kaiser Wilhelm's delusions of piety and grandeur as he undertook a pilgrimage to the Holy Land appeared in its pages above the pseudonym Hieronymus (Wedekind's regular *nom de plume*) Prussian pride could take no more. Berlin demanded retribution and the offices of *Simplicissimus* were raided. It was a standard rule that all handwritten (and therefore identifiable) material should be destroyed as soon as possible, and so Wedekind was understandably furious to learn that his manuscript had been found. By a stroke of cruel fortune the Munich Schauspielhaus was about to stage a performance of *Erdgeist* and Wedekind saw his chance of establishing himself gone. Local politics, ironically enough, came to his rescue. The Munich authorities were less than pleased to have the Prussians digging around on their territory and consequently dragged their heels in discovering the identity of the poem's author. On the morning of the première it was quietly made known that they expected to have discovered the culprit by the next day! After the performance, at which the play was badly received, Wedekind was shipped off in the early hours of the morning on a roundabout route to Zurich to begin an uncomfortable exile.

Ever ready to jump to conclusions, Wedekind long suspected that Albert Langen, the publisher of *Simplicissimus* (who had made his own escape to Zurich the moment the scandal broke and thence later engineered his own pardon), had deliberately plotted the whole affair to boost circulation, and he settled his account, in part, with an unflattering portrayal of Langen as the publisher Alfred Launhart in the play *Hidalla* (1903) and as a similar figure, Georg Sterner, in *Oaha* (1908).

From Zurich Wedekind moved to Paris, where he spent a miserable time on very little money and eventually returned to Germany in June 1899 to be arrested and imprisoned for *lèse majesté*. It is typical of the man that, although extremely conscious of dates and constantly noting them down in his diaries, he later forgot the one month's remission he received and indicated to Artur Kutscher, his biographer, that he served his full sentence. Kutscher naively believed him, 'releasing' him on 3 March 1900 though Wedekind was in fact released a month earlier.[5] In fairness to Langen it must be said that on this occasion Wedekind's suspicions seem to have been ill-founded, though Langen's actions at the time gave them a measure of credence. Korfiz Holm, a co-editor of *Simplicissimus*, explains in his memoirs[6] that the magazine's legal expert was so amused by the poem that he allowed his sense of humour to cloud his legal judgement, and adds that Langen read him the riot act when the storm broke. Holm has no explanation for the discovery of the manuscript, but ingenuously describes how, in the sure confidence that there would be nothing incriminating there, he opened the very drawer in which it lay and invited the law-officers to search to their heart's content. Such stories, however, have to be taken with a pinch of salt, since Wedekind is surrounded by a legion of apocryphal tales and it is difficult to sift fact from fiction.

In exile in Paris and later in prison Wedekind completed his famous satire of Munich life, *Der Marquis von Keith* (1900), which originally appeared as *Münchener Szenen* (Scenes from Munich). The howls of derision which greeted this work, which is now considered one of his most sophisticated plays, stung Wedekind to bitter reply. His angry feelings are neatly reflected in *König Nicolo, oder So ist das Leben* (King Nicolo, or Such is Life, 1901), the tale of a king overthrown by his bourgeois subjects and eventually, having failed at everything else, forced to play court jester to his own usurper. Nicolo pours out the deep tragedy of his personal situation to find it greeted as high comedy and dies a broken man for whom the last laugh can only come after death.

Consolation of this sort was very necessary for Wedekind at this time. Prison had drained his financial resources and on his release he worked with the then popular cabaret troupes to earn a living. The most famous collaboration was with the *Elf Scharfrichter* (The Eleven Executioners), and while he at first enjoyed the novelty and gratification of public applause for his own work—he was an accomplished recitateur and accompanied his songs with his own compositions—he soon felt more like a performing monkey parading for an audience that ignored his true wares. Once again emotional solace came from a woman, a local girl who was his companion from shortly after his release from prison in 1900 to 1903. She bore him a son, Frank, in May 1902.

By 1904, after a particularly depressing spell, Wedekind's star at last appeared to be rising. He had gained enough self-confidence to appear on stage in his own plays and ensure that his characters were given a valid performance —something that many contemporary actors could not manage—and by 1905 he was able to live off his writing and royalties and give up cabaret appearances. Not that life was straightforward, however: *Die Büchse der Pandora*

(Pandora's Box), the second part of Lulu's career, had appeared in book form in 1904 and sparked off a legal battle that effectively barred the play from public performance during the author's lifetime. The book was seized, and author and publisher charged with propagating immoral material. They were acquitted in May 1905, but the decision was reversed on appeal, and finally in June 1906 the book was banned, but author and publisher acquitted because they had not knowingly proffered immoral material. *Die Büchse der Pandora* then appeared in a heavily modified form to comply with the court's verdict. This, the third edition, was prefaced by a fifty-seven-page foreword repeating the legal judgement that acknowledged Wedekind's serious intent and appealing for a chance to stage the play.

Wedekind was especially bitter at the way the Public Prosecutor had twisted his intentions and he vented his feelings in an unpublished adaptation of Goethe's famous ballad 'Heidenröslein' rendered in the lugubrious prose interpretation of the Public Prosecutor :

> The tramp says: 'I will have sexual intercourse with you, female vagrant.'
>
> The female vagrant answers: 'I will infect you so badly with venereal disease that you will always have cause to remember me.'
>
> Clearly she has no interest in sexual intercourse at that time.

As Wedekind concluded : 'That type of presentation cannot fail to suggest indecency.'[7] The court proceedings dragged on, but in Vienna Karl Kraus put on a private performance of the play in which Wedekind played Jack the Ripper and his future wife, Tilly Newes, was given the rôle of Lulu. After a hectic courtship, during which Tilly attempted suicide, the two were married in Berlin on 1 May 1906. Now at last Wedekind felt he was truly a member of respectable society and that the objections to his person must surely cease. The birth of a daughter Pamela in December 1906 confirmed the strongly bourgeois streak that was always just beneath the surface in him. He became a devoted, doting, over-protective father whose watchful eye began to tell on Tilly, who felt that her approach and competence were being constantly criticised. Both partners found adjustment to marriage difficult and the situation was not eased for Tilly when Wedekind projected their marriage almost transparently on to the stage in his one-act play *Die Zensur* (Censorship, 1907).

The picture of Wedekind that emerges from contemporary accounts of this period is a helpful pointer to the motivation of so many of the characters in his plays. Emotionally Wedekind was extremely vulnerable, and there is evidence in his own notebooks and diaries to suggest that he battled against impotency in his relationship with Tilly. This, after his earlier sexual experiences in Paris and London and the reputation he enjoyed, created a schism between outer and inner reality, which although it had always been present, was now painfully intensified.

His public reputation was that of a man determined to provoke, and at least one of his close friends declined to introduce his sister to Wedekind on the grounds that she would be upset by the question Wedekind invariably posed to young women he met for the first time: 'Are you still a virgin?' To this provocation must be added the deliberately sensual way in which at the end of every other sentence Wedekind would bare his teeth and draw his mouth into a leer, a habit that owed its origin to a much more mundane source. Wedekind had ill-fitting dentures which continually shifted and required readjustment; he developed the gesture to camouflage his embarrassment and reinforce his public image.

As a married man Wedekind was intensely possessive of his 'property', and a man paid Tilly a compliment in his presence at his peril. Wedekind was constantly chasing shadows and found the knowledge of his wife's interesting past often very difficult to bear, and the sight of her acting with other leading men distressed him considerably. Despite this, the actress Tilla Durieux relates[8] how a visitor to the Wedekind apartment could find himself ushered into a strategically placed armchair whence he would find himself staring directly at pictures of Tilly in the nude while Wedekind enjoyed his guest's obvious discomfiture. Wedekind felt secure within the confines of art and was able to taunt with what was 'his', compensating thus for the acute insufficiency and unease he felt in reality. He hated to play second fiddle in any situation. Tilla Durieux recalls occasions when a group of friends were involved in an argument in one of their local haunts and Wedekind found himself at a loss for a cutting reply. He would excuse himself and disappear to the cloakroom, reappearing in a few minutes with a triumphant smile and resume his seat. He would then deliver the perfect answer to the point which had earlier eluded him. By now, of course, the conversation had moved on, and the repartee was hopelessly lost and irrelevant.

There is little wonder that Wedekind's characters are so sensitive to being outmanoeuvred—it was a subject on which Wedekind was an expert. His characters echo Wedekind's need to feel in control and they constantly attempt to rewrite past history in their favour. It is typical of the honesty which Wedekind brought to his work that he was acute enough to see his own failings and to recognise the emotional dynamite and dramatic advantage to be gleaned from his own situation.

Such an emotional and psychological constitution could only provoke marital strain and it was always Tilly who had to make the necessary sacrifices. A second daughter, Kadidja, born in 1911, added to her problems and it is little wonder that she began to suffer bouts of intense depression. Yet it was these facets in Wedekind's character that gave him the insight to write his plays. Max Reinhardt's production of *Frühlings Erwachen* in Berlin in 1906 marked the emergence of Wedekind as a force to be reckoned with, both as a writer and as an actor in his own plays. As an actor Wedekind was a disaster in a Reinhardt production of Molière's *Tartuffe*, but the empathy between himself and his own characters gave his wooden delivery a dynamism and veracity which more than compensated for his technical shortcomings. His performances lacked polish but breathed life.

Financially Wedekind was now quite comfortable, but battles with the censors over each succeeding play imposed a severe strain on him and even more on Tilly who bore the brunt as Wedekind struggled to make his way. Their relationship survived thanks to judicious periods spent apart, but they also made many tours together as guest artists, as Wedekind's plays won increasing acclaim. By 1914, Wedekind's fiftieth birthday, he was sufficiently famous for his friends to organise celebrations and for theatres to put on 'Wedekind weeks' in his honour. An edition of his collected works appeared in six volumes, there was a 'Wedekind-book'[9]—a collection of tributes and critical comment—and, most important of all, a celebration dinner was held in his honour. The prime consideration, noted Thomas Mann, one of the organisers, was that Wedekind should feel that he was getting equal treatment to Gerhart Hauptmann, and Hauptmann had been fêted with a banquet on his fiftieth birthday. The banquet for Wedekind was a great success and he was duly flattered.

The outbreak of World War One shattered all prospects of further improvements. Wedekind's work was banned in some places on the grounds that his plays were not in the public interest, and his income from royalties was decimated. In addition his health was not good, and from then till his death he underwent a number of operations, in between which he recovered sufficiently to appear on stage in tours with Tilly or on his own, leaving her at home with the children.

Tilly found it increasingly difficult to accept the rôle that Wedekind's need for constant reassurance demanded she play in their relationship and Wedekind himself provided the straw that broke the camel's back. Flushed with success from the Berlin run in *Lulu* with Maria Orska, he threw Tilly's depressions back in her face: 'If I can act with other actresses, I don't need you at all.'[10] The prospect of a renewed personal battle was too much and Tilly took a dose of mercury tablets. When discovered, she was placed first in an institution and then in a private clinic and was barely discharged from hospital when her husband died. Wedekind had found the rupture that had plagued him increasingly difficult to bear, and seized on the absence of his regular surgeon to undergo an operation with a different doctor. This was performed on 2 March 1918, but complications set in and Wedekind died a week later on 9 March.

2

THE MAJOR THEMES

From the start, criticism of Wedekind's work in the theatre was bedevilled by the author's participation as an actor in his own plays. This often suggested parallels between events on stage and in Wedekind's personal life or could be interpreted in confessional terms. In one sense Wedekind *was* dealing in autobiography, in that he was keenly aware of the parasitic nature of the artist's way of life, and he projected this unease into his characters. If he chose details that had their origins in his own life, it was because he was an acute observer rather than an original thinker. His innovations lie in the choice of subject matter and the way in which he presents his material, and in both cases Wedekind is reacting against the contemporary situation rather than founding a new style. He viewed attempts to present his works in the Expressionist mode with extreme disfavour. Where he scores is as a commentator whose sharp eye for the dramatic is matched by a keen awareness of hidden motives and of implications behind the words of a verbal exchange.

In any study of Wedekind it is crucial to listen to the 'sub-text' as well as to what is actually being said. He strives to reveal the essentially competitive nature of social intercourse; much of the source material was very close to his personal situation, and when he drew on friends and acquaintances he was able, in his own mind, to detach the event from the individual; the former he clearly regarded as common property and suitable for dramatic exploitation.

The fact that, though his plays now lack biographical immediacy, they still provide gripping theatre, is proof of Wedekind's dramatic acumen, if cold comfort to his victims at the time. When he began his play *Musik* (Music) in 1906 he based it on an abortion-ring scandal that had filled the Munich papers for several weeks.

The play's publication in June 1907 effectively pilloried one of the participants in the affair, an acquaintance of Wedekind's, who as a consequence had to give up his post as music teacher at the Munich academy. Some little time later the two met and Wedekind was taken aback at the reception he received. He wrote in a letter to Tilly, dated 21 July 1907:

> The meeting with Dressler was very awkward, as things are going badly for him in every respect. He has lost his position at the Academy and hasn't yet read the play.

The naiveté that caused him to believe that Dressler would be more understanding once he *had* read the play is characteristic; so is the fact that Wedekind offered Dressler half the royalties from the play, an offer Dressler refused. Wedekind constantly collected events and personalities and stored them away for future use; he seemed to be quite blind to the hurt this caused his victims, though he himself had been the first to protest when he was on the receiving end in Hauptmann's *Das Friedensfest*.

Tilly Wedekind sums her husband up well when she says that he *lived* only with and in his characters, and in real life lost the psychological empathy that enabled him to create such gripping theatrical moments.[11] In life Wedekind was often as naive and vulnerable as a child. The empathy that flowed between author and characters stemmed from their common situation. There is little doubt that Wedekind felt deep sympathy for the attitude his characters presented, while his social convictions required that he expose the same characters as self-deluded shadows of humanity. The deep sincerity with which Wedekind's characters profess their philosophical, moral or artistic views is often all too evident, but the author ensures that this sincerity is placed in a true context and tested in social situations where, more often than not, it emerges as desperate self-interest and special pleading.

This is particularly true of the artist. In the sultry atmosphere of Wedekind's plays the artistic pursuit and its equivalent prevarications are demonstrably sterile, self-indulgent and socially objectionable; the adherents of such a way of life are invariably shown on the path to self-destruction. For this reason Walter Sokel's assessment of Wedekind in *The Writer in Extremis*[12] misses the real issue, for Sokel's thesis requires Wedekind to be presented as a writer of confessional documents on the plight of the artist misunderstood and neglected by a hostile and uncomprehending public. Such an approach ignores the satirical element of Wedekind's technique, for the plain fact is, that where his artists are failures, it is because they deserve to fail, and the much-maligned public is shown to have more sense than might at first sight be apparent.

Since the figure of the artist, the artistic hanger-on, and all the many habitués of the artistic world (speculators, angels, financiers, tired businessmen, etc.) are the most frequent characters in Wedekind's plays it is as well to understand why they are there. This was the stratum of society that Wedekind knew best and could most effectively translate into his work, but the essence of the artistic world is its difference to the bourgeois way of life : one cannot be an artist *and* a full, normal member of society. The rôle of the artist in society is nebulous, he is more tolerated than accepted. The characters who, in Wedekind's plays, live on the fringe of society, do so because they cannot exist within a society where they are made to feel inferior, insecure or simply inadequate. Society refuses to allow them the life style they feel is their due, and it consistently destroys the illusions they create for themselves. In sheer self-interest they then retreat as far as is necessary while staying as close to society as possible. For all their grand talk and condescension to the 'common mass' they are where they are because there is nowhere else for them to go, and since they long for a secure social position they attempt to reconstruct social conventions in their own actions and relationships.

Since it is society itself which regards the artistic world as a world apart Wedekind may be quite ruthless in his criticisms of the artistic community without appearing to attack society. He sees the artistic world as a microcosm of society and it is society at large with its taboos, hypocrisies and conventions that is Wedekind's real target. Within the framework of the artistic world Wedekind can better isolate the effect of these factors and present them more graphically to his respectable bourgeois audiences. The Swiss writer Friedrich Dürrenmatt, an enthusiastic admirer of Wedekind, said of his own work: 'Comedy is a mousetrap'.[13] Wedekind, too, lures his audience on. Only when the bait is swallowed and the artistic world self-righteously condemned is the audience guided to a realisation that there is *no* difference between the artistic way of life presented on the stage and its own life.

Wedekind's artists fail, not because they fall foul of the practices of bourgeois society, but because they carry them out to the letter in an environment where the inhuman and unfeeling basis of these practices is all too apparent. The artist-figure and his parallel manifestations are the means to an end in Wedekind's work. They are searching for happiness and a sense of personal freedom in which they may fully express their own personalities and 'be themselves'. Unfortunately, however, society has so distorted the standards of the individual that self-expression assumes the guise of self-assertion at the expense of someone else. Twisted and deformed by the society which surrounds them and which Wedekind holds accountable, his characters lack an understanding of real happiness and equate it with an outward show of superiority or the ability to impose one's will on others. This is an all-pervasive attitude, Wedekind believes, but is particularly clear-cut in society's ambivalent, hypocritical and degrading attitude to sexual mattters.

Wedekind's presentation of sexual confrontations has long caused controversy. In the early days, a critic who approved of Wedekind hailed him as an emancipator of the flesh, if he did not, he condemned him as a purveyor of infamy. This is too simplistic a view, for Wedekind uses sex as he uses the figure of the artist: as a means to an end. His intention is to expose the inherent lack of human dignity and self-respect that was part and parcel of the society of his day.

In the short story *Die Schutzimpfung* (The Inoculation, publ. 1903) marriage and infidelity are reduced by the attitudes of the participants to the level of a locker-room anecdote. Fanny, an attractive young lady who is having an affair with one of her husband's friends has devised a foolproof scheme to keep the relationship a secret. She announces at frequent intervals that it is only thanks to the friend that she has not yet committed adultery but that given half a chance she would not resist him. One day the husband arrives at his friend's house to find him in bed with Fanny, who disappears beneath the bedclothes while the friend tries to get rid of the husband before he recognises her clothes on the chair. Clamping his hand firmly over Fanny's mouth the friend pulls back the duvet from the foot of the bed till all that remains hidden of Fanny is her face. The husband departs in good humour, complimenting his friend on his taste, and later informs Fanny that their friend's lack of interest in her is due to a mistress who is far more attractive than she ever was. The story is told in an anecdotal fashion and the atmosphere of a risqué joke which sustains it implies the wealth of social criticism beneath the surface.

Wedekind's diaries and notebooks offer ample proof of his ability to devise detailed sexual fantasies as well as a keen interest in every aspect of sexual behaviour, but time and again the sexual standards that are depicted as socially acceptable prove to be cold, inhuman and destructive. Even the incomplete manuscript drafts of *Die grosse Liebe* (Great Love, *c*.1906) which contain an explicit, detailed account of mass public sexual intercourse, flagellation and similar rites appear to be the impersonal 'social' backcloth against which a personal view of the participants is to be set. Only on the individual level, in the unfinished account of a figure who has to some extent rebelled against the system, is there any warmth and humanity. It is as if Wedekind had created a monstrous parody of social ritual in order to destroy both the reflection and the image.

In the published work sex is primarily presented by implication and suggestion. The fire-raiser who tells his story in *Der Brand von Egliswyl* (The Fire at Egliswyl, 1895–96) describes his entry into various bedrooms, but the extent of the passion which drives him to set fire to his village when he feels slighted is conveyed by implication, not least because it is not understood by the narrator himself. Where sex is explicit, as in the masturbation race in *Frühlings Erwachen*, it is there to forestall a conventional reaction on the part of Wedekind's audience. Even the various brothel settings in the plays and stories serve the same end.

The prostitute in the story *Das Opferlamm* (The Sacrificial Lamb, 1895–96) is obliged by a sadistic client to bare her soul and reveal why she came to the brothel. Stunned by what he hears, the roué learns a lesson he will never forget: 'He had learnt to believe in innocence, where he had never thought to look for it. He despised himself every time he thought of the girl after that.' (GW I, 273). The play *Das Sonnenspektrum* (The Rainbow, 1894), 'An Idyll of Modern Life', begins by seeming to glory in sexual freedom, but as the audience listens to the reasons why clients and girls are in the brothel the utter emptiness of social life and the characters' inability to cope with it without some convenient bolt-hole is evident. In *Tod und Teufel* (Death and the Devil, 1905), a confrontation between a procurer Casti-Piani and an ardent spinsterly fighter against prostitution is set against a dialogue between prostitute and client which shatters the self-centred beliefs of both protagonists and culminates in Casti-Piani's suicide. The frigidity in the relationships which Wedekind portrays in works like these contributes considerably to the cruel, inhuman atmosphere of his plays as a whole. As Franz Blei's contribution to the *Wedekindbuch* has it:

> These insatiably predatory females seem to spend their lives with their legs apart, but it is a sight more likely to appeal to a gynaecologist than a lover.[14]

There is no warmth in Wedekind's work because very few characters have the capacity to show or feel it. His characters, unable to achieve a harmonious human relationship with its demands of give and take, confront each other in more or less open conflict. Yet it would be misleading to define these relationships as the law of the jungle, for that presupposes a conflict between wild, free, powerful animals; rather we should turn to the convention and routine of the circus for the paradigm. Here the participants are shadows of their natural potential, a mockery of their true selves and it is society which has so reduced them.

THE MAJOR THEMES

The words of the Ringmaster in the Prologue to *Erdgeist*, so often quoted to illustrate the vitality and sexual potency of Wedekind's world, need to be carefully measured against their context. The circus-flavour provides a fitting introduction to life in the raw though there is no true continuity between prologue and play other than the sense of the inhuman spectacle that is imminent. In the Prologue, which was not staged until the tenth performance of the play, the Ringmaster boldly harangues his audience:

> These comedies and tragedies—what can they offer? House-trained pets with such *nice* natures, cooling their ardour on lettuce-leaves and revelling in gossip—just like the audiences that watch them. Here's one who can't drink schnaps and another who doubts he can love. It takes the next one five weary acts to learn he can't cope with life and there's no-one to put him out of his misery! A real beast, a wild, beautiful beast—ladies—you can only see *that* here! (GW III, 8)

This claim, which allowed Wedekind a much cherished disparagement of the Naturalists and Gerhart Hauptmann, has led critics to seek the wild, beautiful animal in characters like Lulu and Dr. Schön who inflate their self-importance with scant regard for the niceties of accuracy. Lulu is offered here to the ladies as an encouragement and example, but in the event neither she nor her patron Schön have real vitality; though the pace and tone of their inevitable collapse differs markedly from the mood of a Naturalist play, in essence they share many similarities with the characters in Hauptmann's work. No circus-barker, though, will admit that *his* fine beasts are toothless wonders; in the interest of his livelihood and self-respect he will embellish what he has to offer, no matter how accurately he may depict his rivals' attractions. Many of Wedekind's characters share this ability to characterise others while failing to see the beam in their own eye. It is a recurrent weakness that is the cause of their undoing.

3

THE THREE-RING CIRCUS

(i) The Travelling Circus:
Fritz Schwigerling oder Der Liebestrank

Wedekind's enthusiasm for the circus is well-known. He wrote pantomimes for circus performance and revelled in all aspects of the circus world. One of his earliest published essays reflects this interest. Written in Zurich in 1887 and called 'Zirkusgedanken' (Reflections on the Circus), it draws a direct parallel between the circus and society which can be traced in Wedekind's work even when the circus world is not explicit. Wedekind admired physical prowess and the beauty and skill of circus artistes, but his admiration was limited to the arena and he was unimpressed by any attempts to trade on that glory outside its due context.

Through the medium of the circus Wedekind found a clearly definable paradigm for society's own false premises, and in this essay he compares the breath-taking gyrations of the trapeze artist with the often less spectacular and superficially less impressive movements of the tightrope walker. The difference lies, he suggests, in the fact that the bravura performances of the trapeze artist are in the main due to the anchor-points which support the trapeze. So long as these hold and the artiste keeps her grip all is well. If the anchor points fail there is nothing the artiste can do to prevent a fall. The tightrope walker, on the other hand, though less eye-catching, performs simply by staying on the high wire. She is much more dependent on her own skill and her movements and ability to impress are necessarily more restricted.

Despite the over-simplifications involved—and Wedekind carefully places his argument in the mouth of a Doctor of Philosophy, Second Class—the comparison is helpful. For the most part Wedekind's characters are like the trapeze artist; they have discovered some protective illusion or fixed point that sustains them and encourages them in delusions of grandeur and a misplaced sense of well-being. They do not see the weakness of their position, or choose to ignore it. They are so taken up with their illusions that even when they fall there is a safety-net beneath them and they bounce back to start again. They manufacture a scenario for themselves that will survive for as long as they are able to maintain the arbitrary fixed points of reference which protect them, and they bounce back not through fortitude but in desperation. Wedekind's characters cannot admit failure to themselves and they constantly find themselves forced to adapt to new circumstances in order to conceal their inadequacy from themselves and others.

Success in the circus depends on the ability to think quickly and act decisively. Panache, showmanship, breathtaking *tours de force* are the order of the day, and success attends only those who can accomplish them. Emotion has no place in the circus arena, there is no time for feelings —the show must go on. Consequently, within the clear-cut conventions of the circus ring the emotionally weak and insufficient may hide their inadequacy behind a slick routine and still feel a personal success as they bask in the audience's applause, transferring it in their own minds from their skill as an artist to their qualities as a human being.

In the conventions of a farce such as *Der Liebestrank* (The Love-potion, 1891–92) Wedekind can use the distance from reality to present and comment on the motivations of such characters, introducing devices of double-talk, cross-talk, slapstick, verbal puns and incredible complications of plot to highlight a situation that, though still present, is less obvious in a realistic setting. After *Der Liebestrank* for example, Wedekind returns to a more sober contemporary setting for *Lulu* which he shows to be as farcical in its essence as is the Russian estate of Prince Rogoschin which is the setting for *Der Liebestrank*.

Prince Rogoschin is a man past his prime who retains delusions of his capacity as a Don Juan and memories of his youth in Moscow to sustain himself. The love-potion in question is the reason why a circus-artiste, Fritz Schwigerling, has been brought to the estate, ostensibly to tutor the prince's children. In fact Rogoschin has taken a decided fancy to his own young and attractive ward Katharina, and since her complete indifference to his advances proves unshakeable, he has brought Schwigerling to his estate in the mistaken belief that the latter possesses gypsy blood and will therefore be able to brew a love-potion to make Rogoschin irresistible. The concept of a love-potion, a magic, yet tangible talisman to compensate for personal inadequacy and guarantee success is an eminently suitable topic for farce, yet in the later and more serious verse drama *Der Stein der Weisen* (The Philosopher's Stone, 1909) and in less direct allusions in the more social works, Wedekind returns to the need his individuals feel to have some guarantee of their good fortune and success.

Rogoschin's belief in the properties of the potion to rejuvenate him sexually brooks no thwarting, and since Schwigerling, naturally enough, cannot fulfil the demands made on him, he faces a short and uncertain future. His is the archetypal situation for a character in Wedekind's world. He is placed in a situation which is beyond his capacity to withstand and desperately tries to conceal his insufficiency. The clear-cut conventions of farce allow Schwigerling's situation a harmless turn, but the infrastructure recurs in a more drastic form in the Lulu plays, in *Der Marquis von Keith* and *König Nicolo*.

Schwigerling uses the aura and ethos of the circus world as a magic cloak to help him attain and maintain a superior position to those about him and to keep up his own spirits. When the prince visits the cellar where Schwigerling is locked up till he produces the potion, he finds the artist resplendent in full magician's rig complete with magical characters on his costume.

> *Rogoschin:* You seem well versed in these matters.
> *Schwigerling (with a glance at his costume):* It's a question of confidence. It just doesn't feel right in a frock-coat.
>
> (II,5; GW II, 210)

The verbal comedy reflects an unspoken philosophy. Schwigerling carries the circus with him wherever he goes, because within its framework he *knows* he is a success. If he can extend the realm of his art to incorporate social encounters as well, he is convinced he will both maintain and extend this success. The confrontation with Rogoschin over the love-potion shows how empty this ploy really is. Since this is a farce we can laugh, but the comedy darkens in Wedekind's social plays. The clarity of motivation that farce allows presents a glimpse of the way his characters' minds work which is relevant to the later works also. The black comedy we find in *Lulu* combines the pathos of Schwigerling's approach to life with the grimmer overtones of reality.

In the characters of *Der Liebestrank* Wedekind presents figures who have escaped from overpowering demands of life into a more congenial atmosphere; even Schwigerling was pleased enough to accept the post of tutor since he had just quarrelled with his previous employer. The most striking refugee is Rogoschin's manservant Cölestin, and in true farce style he and Schwigerling discover they are long lost friends. Lebœuf (alias Cölestin) was a leading actor in the provinces who graduated to Paris and had to content himself with supporting rôles and bit parts:

> *Cölestin:* Paris had nothing to offer me but bread, and you can't live on bread. If I had stayed with the Théâtre Français they would have made me a nobody. . . . In the meanwhile I had the chance to master the rôle of the perfect manservant. Prince Rogoschin engaged me warm from the stage, so to speak. . . . There I was in a comedy by Molière, fighting a duel on behalf of a fool of a master and dying a heroic death to thunderous applause. 'You don't find servants like that every day,' he said, and offered me my present situation. (I,7; GW II, 187)

The comedy of such a deliberate (or unwitting) elision of the discrepancy between illusion and reality is the essence of farce; secure in his stage rôle Cölestin could effect a successful exchange of rôles, so that for him the 'play' has become the 'reality' of work on the Rogoschin estate. This is but one step away from the situation of *Der Kammersänger* (The Court Singer, 1897) in which the tenor Gerardo finds himself obliged to continue his rôles as Tannhäuser and Tristan off-stage as well as on if he is to maintain his public image and the consequent freedom of movement which his emotional sterility cannot achieve in any other way.

Schwigerling's superiority has in fact been destroyed even before the audience has seen him. Katharina, the source of all his embarrassment, spends her time riding the prince's horses into the ground in an attempt to work off her energies and bitterly berates him for the lack of quality in his stables. Her latest ride, she complains, has just dropped exhausted to its knees in the middle of the village: 'And then some schoolmaster comes along and helps it back on its feet.' (I,5; GW II, 182). Schwigerling tells it slightly differently (I,13; GW II, 195) but Katharina has presented him as one who, despite his claims to artistry and expertise, has 'schoolmaster' in his every feature. His debonair condescension to Cölestin, the bluster of the adventurer who has no roots, cuts no ice with the manservant who is all too aware of the harsh reality behind the façade and has his own niche:

> *Schwigerling:* We have no home, no possessions, but in their place Heaven has given us that daemonic Je ne sais quoi. . . .
> *Cölestin:* You can keep your je ne sais quoi. I can do without that.
> *Schwigerling:* That's still no reason to demean yourself and become a lackey.
> *Cölestin:* Being a lackey is a hundred times better than being a schoolmaster.
>
> (I,13; GW II, 197)

Where the servant at least accepts his rôle, the implication is that the schoolmaster is constantly obliged to compensate for a deep-felt sense of insecurity by asserting his dominance on those under his tutelage who, by definition, are more malleable and complaisant. Once again this situation recurs throughout Wedekind's work; the echoes of the circus ring help reveal its true bias.

Schwigerling finds that all his circus expertise is of little value now he is outside the arena, and so he falls back on the only viable means open to him of redressing the balance:

> I'll write a play about all this! In three acts. In every language there is; *and* I'll play the title rôle myself—in every language in the world! When the world learns what princes are like in Russia, it won't know which way to turn. (III,1; GW II, 228)

In reality it is Schwigerling who doesn't know which way to turn to retrieve the situation. As the author of his play he would have been able to reduce the forces that threaten him to manageable proportions, and by playing the title rôle would have emerged the victor. Such a victory is possible only in art; once he leaves his circus environment Schwigerling's vulnerability is all too apparent. Here the dilemma and its resolution are comic, but *Die Zensur* traces an almost identical pattern with tragic consequences, revealing the parallel attractions of the circus and the artistic environment with striking clarity. Though by no means all of Wedekind's characters wish to write plays, they each have their own fixed image of how things are, are going to be, or were, in order to explain away their present precarious situations. The comedy of farce mirrors the tragedy of human inadequacy.

As refugees from the challenges of life Wedekind's characters seek objectively recognised standards against which they may measure themselves and be seen to be measured. Katharina has never found any self-knowledge nor has she had the opportunity to develop normally, so she is readily seduced by the lure of the circus (as expounded by Schwigerling) and its promise of the one thing she has never known: physical freedom. In contrast, Rogoschin's wife Cordelia (who, it transpires, was Schwigerling's *first* wife) evinces a serenity and calmness in the midst of the frenetic comings and goings of the play that has only one possible source. Cordelia knows exactly what she is worth and what she has meant to the men who have passed through her life. Her readiness to be bought and sold (Rogoschin purchased her as the 'Virgin of Colorado River' for $150,000) reflects a universal need for tangible values. Cordelia knows her worth to the last digit and as a result has a considerable advantage and total self-possession in her dealings with the rest of the household.

Once again Wedekind manipulates the explicit possibilities of farce to reveal a standard which prevails implicitly in more 'normal' social situations. Rogoschin demands a love-potion but Schwigerling too needs an elixir of life to restore his fading youth, and he finds it in Katharina. In this relationship Wedekind indicates how it is Katharina's temporary weakness that gives Schwigerling his position of strength. She refuses to help him placate the prince until he agrees to give her what she needs; she is not seduced by Schwigerling's personality, to which she is as unflatteringly resistant as she was to Rogoschin's advances, but by the artist's promise of an introduction to the circus.

Schwigerling deludes himself if he bases her companionship on what he *is* rather than on what he does. He cannot hope to keep pace with Katharina as she develops, and he will soon find that the world will once more intrude into his private scenario and remind him yet again of his basic inferiority. Schwigerling's aura of mastery stems from his virtuosity in the circus, and he relies on the circus to sustain him :

> There's not a bone in my body that's not been broken, but show me a situation I cannot master. That's what you learn in the circus. A decisive leap, and an elegant knee-bend as your feet touch the ground, then you'll not fall on your face. Everyone trips up now and again in the dark, but if you can't spring back up again you'll be trampled flat in the rush—and no-one will care. (I,13; GW II, 197)

Schwigerling leaves the Rogoschin estate with Katharina bubbling with confidence—an apparent proof of the powers of the circus ethos. However, Schwigerling retreated to the estate in the first place because he no longer felt able to face up to the world outside. As the farce develops Wedekind seeks to keep the audience aware of this fact; Schwigerling's 'escape', as he himself well knows, takes him from the frying pan into the fire.

(ii) The Social Circus:
Der Kammersänger; Die Zensur

The tone adopted in *Der Liebestrank* is inevitably muted when Wedekind applies the implications of the circus world to more realistic milieus, but even in *Der Kammersänger* (The Court Singer, 1897) the same prevarications that characterised Cölestin and Schwigerling are present. The circus has still come to town, only now its attraction is Gerardo, a leading Wagnerian tenor, who is making a provincial tour of 'guest appearances'. The social circus, as shown by Wedekind through this play and *Die Zensur* (Censorship, 1907) is also characterised by an inability to show and feel true emotion, so the ground rules of the successful circus performance still hold good.

Wedekind aptly described this play in a preface as 'the confrontation between brutal intelligence and a sequence of blind passions' (GW III, 197), a phrase equally applicable to the ringmaster and his performing animals: intellect versus instinct. The circus world, which reflects in its performances the two sides of human nature—the need to dominate and the need to be dominated—is echoed in the activities of society, and may be used as a convenient alibi for personal weakness. The selfless, total dedication demanded of all circus artistes if they are to survive now appears as a sacrifice made to a cause or vocation, not least in the picture Gerardo paints of himself as a slave to his art. Subservience to an abstract ideal is a ready means of evading emotional involvement or personal responsibility for one's actions. Given the way that society has drained each individual of the capacity for personal thought and moulded him to conform to a pattern, those characters who find themselves out of their depth readily translate their insecurity into a fanatical dedication to their ideal. Since Wedekind feels that society rather than individual weakness bears the prime responsibility for this condition, he paints a picture of a society tainted by this general malaise. In a society as acquisitive and aggressive as the one Wedekind portrays there is no room for private sensibilities. Gerardo moves from one 'guest appearance' to the next, he is contractually bound to put himself at the service of his art, and this requirement is his lifeline.

Der Kammersänger, a one-act play, is set in Gerardo's hotel room as he finishes his packing before moving on to his next engagement, *Tristan* in Brussels. Before he can leave, however, he is faced with three intruders who have eluded the hotel staff and confront him in turn with their demands. The play derives its tension and kinetic energy from the cumulative effect of these increasingly menacing challenges. The first visitor, a swooning teenager, Miss Coeurne, is easily despatched with a signed photograph of Gerardo. The second, Professor Dühring, a white-haired composer whose music lies unread and unperformed in the cupboards of opera houses all over Germany, obliges Gerardo to retreat more conspicuously into the protection of his art. Gerardo invokes his rôle as a professional singer employed to sing and not to make critical judgements. The crucial and direct assault in this swift-moving play comes from Helene Marowa, the town beauty, with whom Gerardo has been having a brief affair. Where Gerardo feels that he has come to the end of the 'guest appearance', she has taken events much more to heart and will not let go. Rather than live without him and return to a drab reality Helene commits suicide, leaving the singer to extricate himself as best he may.

Gerardo regards himself as a 'professional artist' (4; GW III, 209)—an unfortunate phrase for him, since it precisely reveals the flaw in his character. He has made his art his life and his life his art. In his rôle on stage as Tannhäuser, as he patiently explains to the moonstruck Miss Coeurne, he is *supposed* to make his public swoon: 'Is it my fault you have fallen in love with me? Everyone does that. That's what I am there for.' (GW III, 210). So, when the audience hears him give Miss Coeurne his 'word as an artist' (GW III, 209) it is worth remembering that it is the word of one reluctant to reach out beyond the orchestra pit lest he be caught off-balance. Gerardo's tactful and fatherly handling of Miss Coeurne is presented by Wedekind in such a way that the audience will approve of the singer's actions and tend to side with him in his dealings with Dühring. Only the advent of Helene reveals the inherent falsity of the position Gerardo has adopted and demands a reassessment of his motives.

Professor Dühring is a stronger threat than Miss Coeurne. Here the artist who has made art his profession is faced by one who has made his art his life, or so it seems. In fact, the distinction between Gerardo and Dühring is that between success and failure, between acceptance and rejection by society. This distinction is grounded solely in the fact that Gerardo is a performer of others' works while Dühring has to rely on his creative inventiveness. The singer has avoided the composer's dilemma by subjugating his personality to the judgement of those who pay, or who are paid, to decide what is 'good' and what they want to hear. His security derives from an acceptance of the prevailing standards of society and he prospers because he is a mouthpiece for what is socially and artistically safe and accepted. For Gerardo true values come from the wallet and their virtue is their tangibility:

> If I earn half a million then it is because through me that a legion of taxi-drivers, writers, dressmakers, market-gardeners and innkeepers can earn a living. Money flows. People feel the blood pulsing through their veins. . . . It's the world that tells you what a person is worth, not personal convictions, nursed and nurtured over the years. I did not try and sell myself on

the open market; I was discovered. There is no such thing as a neglected genius. (7; GW III, 225)

Money has a clear-cut value which allows both sides of a transaction to know where they stand:

> It is easy enough to gain recognition if it's given for free. Since I was fifteen I have been paid for everything I have done. I would have been ashamed to work for nothing. (GW III, 223)

The sense of security that Schwigerling sought to transfer from the circus arena is available to an artist like Gerardo from the box-office. Similar security and self-awareness is available to a bride through her dowry, a speculator through his profits and a prostitute by the fee she agrees with her client. The security of action and reaction, which is the aim of these varying manifestations of social activity, is well put by one of the clients of the brothel in *Das Sonnenspektrum*: 'I can behave as I like here, I don't have to ask if it is polite.' (GW IX, 146).

In contrast to Gerardo, Dühring believes in the merit of his own work with a faith that defies public and critical indifference: it is the sole source of his strength to continue. Wedekind allows Dühring to play a few snatches from his work so that his audience may hear how patently he deserves to be ignored and how right Gerardo is to have nothing to do with him. Once again the author disarms such suspicions as the audience might have begun to harbour so that the final confrontation may be all the more effective.

Dühring wants artistic recognition *and* material security without having to accept the standards of a materialist society, and herein lies his relevance to Gerardo who is also using his art as a compensation for his own inadequacies. Gerardo can mask his personal insufficiency behind his rôle as an artist who is paid to perform certain limited functions within which he is contractually bound to remain

—and he can look to his financial resources for the reassurance he seeks that his is a worthwhile way of life. Money is the means to an end: the sense of security derives from his artistic performance. However, Dühring's appearance places Gerardo in another recurrent situation in Wedekind's work: the critical moment when an individual is forced to question the way of life that has sustained him up to that moment. Though the social realities enable Gerardo to fob Dühring off, the old man has confused him and made him stop and think. As a result Gerardo is confused and off-balance when the third, compelling challenge sweeps in in the shape of Helene Marowa.

The difference between Dühring and Helene as opponents is that the former plays by rules of which the latter professes ignorance. Gerardo's contract explicitly forbids him to travel in the company of women or to marry; it consequently allows him to flirt with the women in the towns he visits and, indeed, half his attraction for them would be lost if he did not have this freedom. The pathos of the situation is clear: Helene is prepared to abandon her bourgeois way of life for Gerardo, and he too would like to break out of the rut he has made for himself, but lacks the strength to defy the standards that have sustained him for so long. In Gerardo Helene sees a man whose value and position is precisely known and in whom she feels she cannot be deceived as she was in her marriage. It is Gerardo's necessary task to wean her away from this delusion without damage to his public image.

Gerardo is all too well aware that Helene's marriage contract outbids his artistic contract in society's eyes, and that if there is a scandal it will destroy him. He is thus trapped into admitting to himself that the security he sought in his art, and which sufficed for Miss Coeurne and Dühring, must give way in a direct assault from a social institution. As with Dühring Gerardo tries to accept this without a painful loss of self-esteem by turning to the basis of materialism and constant values that is his way of life. His security is dependent on his ability to remain free of such small-mindedness as 'love':

> If *I* sell myself then at least I do it honestly! ... *Love* is a haven for cowards and stick-in-the-muds. In the world at large where I move everyone knows what everyone else is worth. If two people come together they know exactly what to expect from each other. They don't need *love*! (9; GW III, 238)

His relationship with Helene was part of his 'guest appearance'; he was drawn into the affair by the same needs that led him into an artistic career in the first place —a reluctance to offend prevailing customs and a need to inflate his own ego; only now does he discover that Helene and he talk the same language but mean different things. Having given Helene the illusion of freedom she sought but cannot translate into reality, Gerardo is convinced that he has fulfilled the requirements of society. On stage as Tannhäuser there is no question of responsibility for the way people react to him, off stage (if indeed such a state exists for Gerardo) the artist may hide behind his contract which requires him to live out his rôle in his social encounters. Gerardo is constitutionally incapable of breaking this contract, while Helene cannot break her marriage contract and remain within society. The impasse that ensues illustrates Wedekind's sense of the shallowness of a society that lives and breathes by material standards; Gerardo and Helene are victims of a conspiracy in which they are willing partners, but they had no alternative. Helene's drab home life and her marriage gave her the necessary security against which she can safely daydream, and Gerardo's artistic rôle is to foster this need so that it may safely be indulged in without destroying the fabric of society.

It is an ironic comment on the successful presentation of art in the manner of Gerardo that Helene arrives with a pistol concealed in her bag, clearly determined to play out a melodrama of her own and die the death of a lovelorn heroine. Not for the first or the last time Wedekind destroys the distinction drawn on-stage between art and life to show their true similarity. Helene's final movements are so swift and unexpected and mark such a break with what has gone before that there can only be one interpretation: she came to Gerardo resolved to die beautifully. Her tragedy and that of so many other weak characters in Wedekind's work is that she cannot recognise the strength of her own feelings. Society has so twisted her values that she can only sense fulfilment in what is an act of utter defeat—for, as the audience has by now realised, Gerardo is not worthy of such a sacrifice.

Helene's death provides Gerardo with a major dilemma: 'If I leave now they'll say I'm a monster, and if I stay I'll have broken my contract. I'll be ruined.' (10; GW III, 240). Gerardo's need, now as ever, is for a *'force majeure'*, as he puts it, that will take responsibility from him. When the search for a policeman to take him into 'protective custody' proves fruitless, he drops Helene to the ground and dashes out in a desperate attempt to take up his next guest appearance.

Gerardo is bound to his artistry as Schwigerling is to the circus. He cannot compete with life on equal terms. His inability to shake himself totally free of his bourgeois origins—he cannot force himself to leave Helene to face up to the numbing emptiness that is the consequence of her own escapism—illustrates the superficiality of his character. Such roots as he has are shallow, and this is the source of both his strength and his weakness: strength because he will always be able to extricate himself from situations which threaten to become emotionally complicated, and weakness because, even though it will be his partners who suffer most, there is a wall between himself and society as impregnable as any that Professor Dühring has to scale. Gerardo survives, but not because he is a figure of light relief. Schwigerling's circus virtuosity has been replaced by an equally insistent emphasis on professionalism, and the darker mood of *Der Kammersänger* throws its shadow over the farce. Gerardo is no spent force, he is a man of intellect who survives by his wits. His sexuality is crucial to his artistic success, and while he may be a shadow of a man in moral terms, there must be no doubt as to his manhood. Wedekind's reaction to early presentations of Gerardo makes this clear: 'Why do they all play Gerardo as if he were a eunuch? There are singers who haven't been castrated.'[15]

The strain of deathly seriousness in all Gerardo undertakes must be apparent in any performance of *Der Kammersänger*. The chilling attraction of the play lies in the combination of tragedy and pathos. Gerardo has a train to catch, and the audience should not be allowed to forget his impatience to get away and put this guest appearance behind him. Gerardo's impatience and his insistence on the need to go stress the sense of routine by which he lives and which has now been suddenly and utterly overwhelmed. Wedekind's projection of his situation not only illustrates the fact that Gerardo has placed the noose about his own neck, but it isolates in clearer relief the relevance of Gerardo's prevarications to that of the society for which Wedekind is writing.

Gerardo's attempts to harmonise the demands of art and life to his personal needs find a revealing counterbalance in the situation presented in *Die Zensur*. In this play, a 'theodicy in one act' (GW V, 105) as Wedekind described it, the stance assumed by the performing artist in *Der Kammersänger* is assigned to a creative artist, the writer Walter Buridan. The setting for the play, Buridan's third-floor apartment in Munich, which affords a 'freer view' (2; GW V, 121) of the city, seems at first to have little in common with a circus arena, but like Gerardo and Schwigerling Buridan has retreated from a hostile world to a sphere where, for at least part of the time, he may live his life in his own way without constant challenge. This recurrent feature in Wedekind's plays finds its most explicit statement in the medieval setting of *Der Stein der Weisen* (The Philosophers' Stone) where the alchemist Basil, beset by the forces of the Church, retreats into his castle and raises the drawbridge behind him. It is an action that would appeal to characters such as Buridan, but in the end Basil's defences prove to be as weak against social challenge as are Buridan's.

The presentation of the circus atmosphere has become more obvious in *Die Zensur* than it was in *Der Kammersänger* and yet it retains a mood of seriousness absent in *Der Liebestrank*. The combination of the two approaches illustrates the inherent bankruptcy in social terms of the mind that can seek to adapt and usurp circus attributes, whether consciously or unconsciously. The play opens with a scene in which Buridan is seen to 'train' his artistic companion Kadidja to perform his songs; there is an explicit reference to the absence of the whip he used in their first lessons together. In the closing sequences, when Buridan has been rejected by society, he makes Kadidja up-end a rolling-drum such as acrobats use in the circus and stand on it while he lectures her as if she were an animal that cannot perform its tricks to his satisfaction. Yet there is no humour in these confrontations, rather the deadly earnest of a drowning man clutching at straws.

Buridan stands at a crucial point in his career, for both his personal and artistic way of life are under attack.

Wedekind was appalled at the exploitation that was such a feature of society and in Walter Buridan he presents a writer in the depths of a personal crisis of his own making. In three closely-related confrontations which follow in rapid succession, Buridan is revealed fighting to maintain the sense of security he mistakenly thought he had already won for himself.

His relationship with Kadidja, the attractive young girl with whom he has been living for the past eighteen months, has reached its lowest ebb, since she is pressing him to marry her and he is most reluctant to take such a drastic step. As a consequence he has lost all enthusiasm for any new work and suffers an additional blow because the censor is withholding the necessary licence that will allow the works he has written to be performed. Buridan faces a direct and sexual challenge from Kadidja whose youthful vitality he now finds overpowering. The social challenge from the office of censor is delivered by the young priest Dr. Prantl. He denies Buridan the one means open to him of redressing his personal inadequacy, namely the 'artistic freedom' that Schwigerling sought when the circus ring proved insufficient, the freedom to reconstitute his life into his art so that he may feel in control of events once more. Buridan is caught in a cleft stick and is finally defeated because his attempts to defuse the challenge Kadidja presents only serve to alienate Dr. Prantl further.

Buridan has started where Schwigerling finished. When he first met Kadidja her youth and inability to cope with life enabled him to rescue her from the 'stormy sea' (3; GW V, 136) and play the socially approved role of guardian and artistic partner. In the past eighteen months Kadidja's function has been to bring life to Buridan's art through their performances together, and, as his creation, to allow the writer to bask in reflected glory at his dominance over one so young and beautiful. Since her rescue, however, Kadidja has found the breathing space she needed and has gradually developed her natural personality from the immature and unnaturally retarded state it was in when she first met Buridan. While still prepared to dance to his tune in his art, she is reluctant to accept the static, subservient rôle he assigns her in their life together. Buridan dare not and cannot draw such a distinction between art and life. He sees his art as a valid mirror of society which exists to reflect with the greatest accuracy what goes on in society, and he places nothing in his art that is not in accordance with his view of life. Consequently his only answer to Kadidja's wish to enhance and complete their artistic partnership with a marital one is to compose a 'wedding ballet' in which Kadidja is cast as bride and given a bridal costume to wear. Buridan is not attempting to deceive her with this offer, he is a victim of self-deception in his concept of art, and it is this self-deceit to which society takes exception, since Buridan's art serves to promote the writer's interests at the expense, if need be, of others. Buridan needs his art to be as realistic as possible so that he may maintain the fiction that while in control of art he is in control of life. To an outsider like Dr. Prantl the resultant impression is less of a play than a series of casualty reports. (2; GW V, 132)

The artist cannot remain forever in an artistic world. Sooner or later he must come into contact with society; the besetting sin of Wedekind's artists, and indeed of the greater part of all his characters, is that they seek to superimpose their view of themselves on to the social framework without making any concessions. They draw distinctions or blur them to suit their own situation, and their motives are continually suspect.

Dr. Prantl's objection to Buridan is less to the content of the writer's work, as Buridan believes, than to the motivation behind it. Prantl is reluctant to licence a writer who lacks integrity and a sense of unity within himself. For all that Buridan proclaims his goal as a writer to be the 'Reunification of Sanctity and Beauty' (2; GW V, 131), Prantl still stumbles over what he terms Buridan's lack of *'anima candida*—the wedding costume which is demanded of the meanest beggar if he is to escape the fires of Hell' (2; GW V, 124). The irony of this statement should not be overlooked. In his choice of expression Wedekind implies that Prantl is as restricted as is Buridan in an insistence on outward visible signs to indicate inner capacities. The Church should be beyond this, but Wedekind neatly indicates the parallelism that exists between the writer and the society that rejects him.

Though Prantl is correct in the inference he draws, his reasons are suspect, and the priest's lack of poise in his unexpected confrontation with Kadidja also serves to place a question mark over his right to dismiss Buridan in the way he does. The writer and priest are in the midst of a long disputation in which Buridan is attempting to justify his approach to art when Kadidja interrupts them. She is wearing, for the first time, the bridal costume for Buridan's wedding ballet. In other words she is dressed as Buridan has 'censored' her to meet his own personal needs. She makes her entrance rolling on her drum and, feeling unsteady, leans on Prantl for support. The costume is described in the stage directions as 'any tasteful imaginative costume' (GW V, 133), but the effect of Buridan's 'censorship' at such close range is to reveal more of Kadidja than normal social intercourse expects, and the priest naturally assumes that Buridan is trying to ensnare him. Though this is not Buridan's intention, the poetic justice of the situation is apparent. Buridan has provoked his own destruction as a writer through the very means by which he hoped to avoid it.

Prantl's abrupt departure is a shattering blow, the more so since the priest states that he no longer takes Buridan seriously. However, his dismissal of the artist because he cannot accept the man is as extreme a view as that which he himself condemns. Wedekind presents Prantl as a man who emerges the victor not through the intrinsic merit of his person or argument but because his is the socially entrenched position. Wedekind reminds his audience of this fact even while he presents in Buridan a writer who deserves his fate.

Once Prantl has left, the truly ruthless element in Buridan's character emerges with all its artistic vigour. He is so conditioned by his own weakness and by the society in which he moves that the only recourse he feels will save his own self-respect is to re-establish his superior position in the best way he can. In Kadidja he has both the cause of his dilemma and the means for its correction. Like all Wedekind's characters he is preoccupied with his own position, he sees his weakness as proof of his partner's strength and so he must destroy her and bring her down to below his level if he is to survive.

Buridan has been censored by society for endangering others, for having a perverting and harmful effect on the unsuspecting member of the public who watches one of his plays, so he immediately arraigns Kadidja in these terms. He attacks her beauty and its effect, for this is where he himself feels vulnerable and inadequate in his relationship with her. With a masterly disregard for the true situation, a characteristic feature of Wedekind's figures, Buridan in his turn adopts the rôle of censor and projects his interpretation of Kadidja's beauty as though it had no relevance to himself:

> Kadidja! When you go out you wear a long dress. You are in no danger so the censor refuses to let you endanger others. As a bareback rider in the circus, however, where a fall means

broken bones, the censor will let you use your body as you please. And if you are a tightrope-walker walking over the market-place from one church-spire to another, you can wear what you like. No censor will worry then. You can clothe your nakedness with a cobweb and he'll not object. Everyone knows that you can't put a foot wrong without crashing to the ground. They'll sweep what's left of you—a mangled unrecognisable mess—into the gutter. (3; GW V, 137)

If Buridan were arguing from within society, such a masterly ability to adjust 'facts' to his advantage would secure his survival. Since he stands outside, his arguments are revealed in their full speciousness.

Buridan has no answer to society's rejection of him other than to retreat deeper into art. He stands Kadidja on her pedestal and regards her as so much 'artistic material' and is oblivious to the human feelings of which she is capable. He humiliates Kadidja so that in despair she throws herself from his balcony to her death. This act, though it frees Buridan of a bond which he found intolerable, leaves him with even more severe restrictions. Society will regard him with even greater suspicion now; his artistic approach to life has claimed a victim, as Prantl saw it would. Buridan has sinned against life and at last falls to his knees and begs forgiveness of his Maker. The question that Wedekind leaves unanswered is, how long will this humility last, can Buridan make a new start. Given the evidence of the play, the answer must tend to the negative. In six months' time Buridan will have fitted his relationship with Kadidja into a new script which presents events in a favourable light. If the worst came to the worst, the rôle of abject penitent rejected by a harsh society would fit the bill.

In *Die Zensur* the explicitness of the circus atmosphere is subsumed under the social arena. Buridan and Schwigerling are two of a kind; they are placed in contrasting situations which illustrate their common failings. Schwigerling succeeds because he is not shown within society, Buridan, and Gerardo in *Der Kammersänger*, fail because the nature of *their* art requires social contact. As an artist Buridan stands vulnerable on the fringe of society, but he is rejected for reasons which have little bearing on the truth of his situation. His defeat is a further indication of the arbitrary nature of the standards of society. Art and society, in Wedekind's presentation, share parallel motives, a situation society is loath to accept. As the artist-figure in Wedekind's work is shown to fail in the end, so Wedekind's intention is to use the artist to confront the members of his audience with the realisation that their own way of life and philosophy are equally bankrupt.

(iii) *Escape from the Circus—Failure and Success: 'Hidalla' oder Karl Hetmann der Zwergriese; Franziska*

Wedekind's characters, while in the main professing to scorn the narrow bourgeois world, secretly envy what they imagine to be the placid security of bourgeois society. They direct all efforts to securing such a position for themselves, which they regard as emanating from the ability of the individual to satisfy the requirements of society without apparent difficulty. Consequently, faced with failure for the umpteenth time, the adventurer, speculator or artist, who a moment before had looked down on the man in the street, now envies those who, to his mind, can consider themselves useful members of society. An early draft for the play *Oaha, die Satire der Satire* (Oaha, Satire on Satire, 1908) set in the offices of the satirical magazine *Till Eulenspiegel* (a *picaro* no less famous than *Simplicissimus*) expresses this attitude well. The speaker is a writer whose job it is to think of dialogue to match the cartoon drawings a colleague has submitted. He is having no success:

A roadsweeper can do what is asked of him, and when he has done it there's no-one in the world can look down on him. When he's finished his work he can go home to his wife and family and enjoy life.[16]

Since by virtue of its mundane, repetitive and unglamorous nature real work is anathema to Wedekind's characters, they must promote their own activities in self-justification and present them to society as worthy of serious consideration. The many parodistic organisations Wedekind invents in his plays reflect this desire to be seen to act 'in the public interest'. Elfriede von Malchus, the spinster who fights to save girls from being lured into prostitution in *Tod and Teufel* (Death and the Devil, 1905), has sublimated her own frustrated sexual desires through her ardent dedication to The International League for the Prevention of Prostitution (GW V, 6); the writer Walter Buridan sees himself as a latter-day John the Baptist preparing the way for the Reunification of Sanctity and Beauty in this world (GW V, 131), and Karl Hetmann in *Hidalla* ('Hidalla' or Karl Hetmann, the Mini-giant, 1903) is the founder of 'The International League for the Propagation of Eugenic Health' (GW IV, 204); his financial backer is Rudolf Launhart who has just established the 'Rudolf Launhart Institute for Social Studies' (GW IV, 192).

Society is readily able to penetrate the crusading veneer of such organisations and expose the self-interest beneath the surface, and yet, as Wedekind strives to show, society itself works to an identical pattern. Society is dependent on group judgements: what the majority does is the norm. With the norm of such group activity removed, the truth emerges and the materialistic bias to life is clearly revealed. This is Wedekind's reason for choosing in his plays characters and situations on the fringe of society. His social satire can bite more deeply and he can hold up to his audience a mirror image of itself which its members will condemn before they realise that they are also condemning their own life-style.

The International League for the Propagation of Eugenic Health is Karl Hetmann's thirteenth attempt to make himself a useful member of society, and is a fine example of misplaced selflessness. Hetmann, an unprepossessing looking individual, toothless, with very little hair and great staring eyes, is obsessed by a profound need to feel he belongs to society. He is touchingly sincere in his attempts to serve his fellow men, and perplexed by society's reluctance to let him help. As the selfless servant of an organisation from which he is excluded and from which he cannot profit personally, he hopes that society will recognise his selflessness and grant him success and social acceptance. Hetmann is searching for an inner meaning to life, committing himself to a cause that will allow him to feel a sense of purpose and dignity. The League has its sole origin in Hetmann's assessment of his personal situation.

In Hetmann's League Wedekind caricatures society's own *mores*. Hetmann's grandiose schemes to improve and foster beauty in the world indicate his awareness of the barriers that have hitherto excluded him. The League is an unwitting parody of the social structure of bourgeois society as seen from the outside and, in attempting to rise above the norms of his day, Hetmann provides the audience with an unflattering reflection of its own way of life. The League is an organisation with entry jealously restricted in an arbitrary fashion which is totally unrelated to personal capacity. It exists to promote and cherish what its members already have (wealth and beauty) and allows its members to pursue self-interest under the banner of social progress. As Hetmann has drawn up the rules of membership, all members of the League have the right and duty

THE THREE-RING CIRCUS 55

to have sexual intercourse with any other member. This is his solution to the sexual taboos and traumas of his age.

This grotesque perversion, which stems directly from Hetmann's idealistic motives, serves to illustrate the extent to which individuals who feel insecure in themselves are led to compensate for this insecurity by attempting to adapt to what they conceive to be prevailing standards. Since their only experience of these standards is at second hand and at a distance, they can only gauge their basis from external appearances. It is this that makes Hetmann's League such a telling comment on society.

Hetmann's idealism is readily exploited by those within the ranks of society. The members of his League are not slow to follow its rules, but Hetmann is betrayed by his own Grand Master who realises that Hetmann's theories will come between himself and the fortune he will gain if he marries another member of the League, the shapely Mrs. Grant. He denounces Hetmann as a madman, as indeed by society's standards he is. In matters of property society knows where to draw the line. Hetmann is equally vulnerable to the activities of his backer, the publisher Rudolf Launhart. Launhart, though not a member of the League, shares two vital qualities with its members; he has position and money. In addition he has the brutal intelligence that characterised Gerardo, but his stronger social position allows him to emerge unscathed from ventures that would defeat the Court Singer.

Launhart's master-stroke has been to marry the daughter of a highly-placed government minister and this gives him a patron and protector. Launhart's wife never appears in the play and he is extremely abrupt whenever she is mentioned. It is as if he would rather not be reminded of the alliance and its implications, but her existence gives Launhart the freedom he needs. He is a born opportunist and thoroughly unscrupulous. The Institute for Social Studies which bears his name is wholly financed by his friend Heinrich Gellinghausen who finds, when he reads the small print of the contract Launhart drew up, that he has signed away his right to ask for his money back. It is Launhart who arrives at the end of the play when Hetmann has committed suicide to take possession of his latest manuscript. Now that the idealist is safely dead the manuscript can be turned into a best-seller and Launhart will make a fortune.

Gellinghausen, a mouthpiece for all the traditional social attitudes, particularly in sexual matters, is well-intentioned, but is the unwitting catalyst for Hetmann's eventual downfall. He has broken off his engagement to Fanny Kettler on learning that she had had an affair with another man before she met Gellinghausen. Fanny is a beautiful, attractive and intelligent woman and as much a victim of exploitation as Hetmann. Launhart depends on her brains and organisational genius to ensure the success of his Institute and as a consequence Fanny has a decisive voice in selecting where the Institute will place its resources. It is in the decision she makes that Wedekind illustrates the way in which society perverts its members. She was incensed at the reasons for Gellinghausen's rejection of her, and turned first to a cause which till then had been as abhorrent to her as it was to Wedekind—the emancipation of women.

After she has heard Hetmann speak, Fanny is fired by his selflessness (in contrast to Gellinghausen's motives) and offers herself as a member of the League. Her enthusiasm is short-lived; she was attracted to Hetmann's ideas on the rebound and for negative reasons. The arrival of Pietro Morosini, the Grand Master of the League, brings home to her the realisation that she has leapt from the frying-pan into the fire. Far from fulfilling Hetmann's description as 'one who combines in his appearance all the qualities in which a man may distinguish himself' (I; GW IV, 207), Morosini appears more a cross between a gigolo and a deb's delight. Hetmann, of course, has studied the attitudes and standards by which society lives and has made his judgement from the practices he has observed as an outsider. In Morosini he found a Grand Master who met all the requirements. Morosini is one of Wedekind's subtler satirical comments on the social ethos.

The ironic and pathetic twist to *Hidalla* is that Fanny falls in love with Hetmann, thus threatening to shatter all his beliefs in human nature and the way of the world. He dare not believe that beauty can love ugliness, for to accept that is to remove the king-pin of his personal alibi for repeated failure. To return Fanny's love Hetmann must abandon and contradict all that he has held dear and that has sustained him for ten years. They are a well-matched pair in fact, for both are searching for a life with meaning, and both are victims of the society in which they find themselves. Fanny's love has brought Hetmann to the point of escaping his own delusions and starting again with eyes that can see beyond the social norm, but such happy endings are not for this world. Society intervenes in its search for material advantage.

Hetmann's interview with the circus impresario Cotrelly, who is looking for an attraction that will outshine a chimpanzee that can sing musical scales, shows him how others see him. Cotrelly offers Hetmann a position as clown, the 'dummer August' (Augustin) who

> falls over every obstacle, always arrives just that fraction too late, tries to help people who can manage ten times better on their own, and best of all, can't see why the audience keeps laughing at him. (V; GW IV, 264)

Despite the fact that Hetmann has begun to see himself in the same light, thanks to Fanny, society has so drained him of the capacity for positive independent thought that he is still oversensitive to the judgement of others. The fear of looking ridiculous is too strong : suicide is the only alternative. There is no doubt that Hetmann's ideas are intended to be rejected by society, but that same society's willingness to see Hetmann in terms of a circus clown is the height of irony. By drawing the threads of the circus world and social practice together in such an explicit and incongruous way Wedekind underlines their common shallowness.

As Hetmann's suicide indicates, Wedekind's characters live in morbid dread of finding themselves in a spotlight on the wrong side of public opinion : in the arena instead of in the auditorium. Their dilemma is made the worse since they can never be sure where the line will be drawn. This constant insecurity is reflected in the lack of dignity and the sense of emptiness which colour Wedekind's works. Given the society in which we live, he suggests, these are the prevarications and defences to which individuals will resort with disastrous consequences to themselves and those about them.

In Wedekind's opinion the sterility of the adult world was caused by pre-adult experience; the prose narrative *Mine-Haha* (Mine-Haha, or On the Physical Education of Young Girls, 1899) provides one illustration, *Frühlings Erwachen* another. *Mine-Haha*, a fresh, spontaneous and naïve memoir of the experiences of a young girl, raises by implication some nagging doubts in the mind of the reader. A young girl arrives safely packed in a tight-fitting box at a white house in a secluded park cut off from the world to be brought up amongst girls only. She describes the education she received in detail and with enthusiasm, and breaks off her story at the moment when she emerges, paired off with a boy of her own age, into the world. She never asks what her education is leading to and she is never told, and if the story lacks a tragic ending it is surely because it breaks off unfinished. Its author, we are told in the introductory framework to the story, has fallen to her death from her upstairs apartment and left the manuscript behind.

Wedekind draws no explicit connection between the frame and the inner story, but a comparison between the two and a direct reference made in the outer frame to *Frühlings Erwachen* as a similar sort of work is enough to cause the reader to look more closely at the idyllic picture painted in the inner story. Retreat into an idyll of one sort or another is generally followed in Wedekind's work by a disastrous re-emergence into reality.

Of all the characters who inhabit Wedekind's work after *Frühlings Erwachen*, only one appears in a truly positive light: the title rôle of *Franziska*, 'A Modern Mystery Play in Five Acts' (1911). Where *Frühlings Erwachen* shows what went wrong, *Franziska* traces the career of a young girl who has shared experiences very similar to those presented in the earlier play but who ultimately comes to a true understanding of herself and finds the rôle in life which is valid for her: that of motherhood. *Franziska* follows the progress of Goethe's Faust in a deliberate twentieth-century parody of man's inability to live within his own limitations and of the restless urge to self-knowledge which when misplaced leaves destruction in its wake.

Franziska Eberhardt, a young middle-class girl dissatisfied with her life, and, thanks to the tensions of her home, emotionally confused and verging on hysterical collapse, has seduced a young man in order to lose her virginity and now wishes to discover what life has to offer her. She receives a nocturnal visitor—via the window—who introduces himself as the impresario Veit Kunz. He offers to engage her as an artist and suggests a pact under whose terms she can have all she desires for the next two years, after which she becomes his. Franziska's demands are clear and categorical: she wants freedom and the ability to enjoy life more than any woman can. If necessary she is prepared to become a *man* in order to gain this desired ability to feel pleasure and have freedom to move.

Veit Kunz: For what you have in mind there is nothing better than an artistic career. Art, you know, can do anything. That's what art is for. If it couldn't, there'd be no sense to it. (I,3; GW VI, 119)

Franziska's desires, so clearly unattainable in this extreme form, are essentially no different from those of most of Wedekind's characters. Her dissatisfaction with a drab bourgeois existence and her desire to experience 'Life' lead to a vivid and grotesque perversion of the natural order of things. Franziska is ready to deny her whole nature to reach her goal, and she finds a conventionally acceptable expression of her wishes through the medium of art.

The pact is made, and Franziska's pilgrimage begins in the 'Wine-Room Clara' in Berlin (*pace* Auerbach's Cellar in Leipzig). She 'marries' a young society girl and their relationship caricatures *mariage à la mode* until Franziska's 'wife' discovers the truth and commits suicide. Wedekind follows Goethe's plot in outline as Franziska's new life develops. There has always been a strong undercurrent of the Faust theme in much of Wedekind's work, here it is explicitly acknowledged and turned to Wedekind's own arguments and manner of presentation.

Franziska is significant not because of its debt to Goethe, but for the totally unexpected mood and tone of its final act. Act Five opens after a lapse of some years and is in complete contrast to the four that preceded it. Franziska has come to terms with herself and turned her back on her previous way of life. The frenetic pace of the first four acts has given place to a steady, even rhythm in keeping with the bourgeois setting: 'A low farmhouse-room with modern fittings' (V,1; GW VI, 206) in the country near Munich. Franziska has found real security as the mother of a four-year-old son, Veitralf, and truly belongs to this setting. She is impervious to the reappearance of two of the men in her past, the actor Ralf Breitenbach and Veit Kunz, both of whom she named as the father of her child. Kunz is now employed as a private detective working for Breitenbach who is convinced that his wife is having an affair; in other words, the world which Franziska left behind still goes on without her.

Now that it no longer matters and Kunz has found himself a rôle to play in society, he has a confession to make to Franziska. The pact they concluded only worked because of Franziska's hysterical condition at the time. His grand bravado was so much hot air:

> When I climbed through your window that summer evening in your mother's house and offered you all that hocuspocus— I was at my wits' end. I had had no luck at all with it on other girls. But the moment I saw you I felt confident, safe, reckless even. As long as I had you with me I knew I was proof against any setback. (V,2; GW VI, 209)

Veit Kunz drew his strength from the natural potential he found in Franziska and turned it to his own ends. He encouraged her in her career because it suited him, and he needed her far more than she needed him. The excesses to which she was led were only possible because her home life had failed to offer her a secure base on which to build and from which she could weather the inevitable storms of life. Now, after all that she has been through, Franziska has found natural fulfilment in her son and with the financial help that comes to her from a wealthy patron she can resume a normal life.

The seal is set on her new-found rôle in a dénouement of such naturalness and cosiness that at first sight it seems Wedekind is parodying himself. Franziska and her child are having their portrait painted by an artist who lives in the same village. The picture, reminiscent of a Madonna and child, is in what might best be called 'Chocolate Box' style with a garland of roses to add the finishing touch. The closing moments of the play have an idyllic quality as Franziska, totally self-assured and composed, is shown in a vision of genuine sentiment rare in Wedekind's work—contented, undemanding and fulfilled. She has had the same morale-boosting effect on the painter Karl Almer that she had on Veit Kunz and the others. This time, thanks to her own self-confidence, she has a positive effect:

Almer: The world is by no means the desperate place the Jonahs would have us believe.
Franziska: Why do they persist in their nonsense then?
Almer (takes Veitralf in his arms and dances round with him): Because they want too much. Isn't that right, Veitralf? Because they don't know their own limitations or those of the world. Men as well as women. We two, we know what we can be for each other!

(V,5; GW VI, 216–17)

As a 'modern mystery play' *Franziska* has moved in form and content away from all claim to reality. The mystery play, like the farce, has its own conventions; it is a parable, a play with a moral. The positive ending of this play implies Wedekind's criticism of the society of his day, for in the more realistic setting of plays such as *Hidalla*, self-discovery and release are impossible. It takes a latter-day *deus ex machina*, the wealthy Baron Hohenkemnath who has taken a fatherly interest in Franziska's fortunes from the start, to assure her the financial security that will guarantee good fortune.

Franziska's counterpart in a realistic setting is the music

pupil Klara Hühnerwadel in *Musik* who also turns her back on art to devote herself to her child. Her fate is to see all her sufferings end in vain: her child dies after a few weeks, and Klara collapses with nervous exhaustion when she sees how she has become a ridiculous pawn in the game of social appearances. Lulu, Kadidja in *Die Zensur* and Effie in *Schloss Wetterstein* (1910) are destroyed because their search for security brought them into contact with the realities of society. Franziska's idyll, then, may be seen either as a pastiche emphasising the hollowness of her asylum when compared to the reality known to the audience, or as a haven where refuge is found after the exertions of a misguided life. Either interpretation is valid and both are tenable concurrently; in the end, the relevance to the 'real world' which Wedekind portrays in his other plays is inescapable.

Franziska is a representative character presented in a stylised mood. Emerging as she did from a labyrinth of inexplicable emotional confrontations within herself and in her parents' relationship, she directly parallels the more sober version presented in *Frühlings Erwachen*. In *Franziska* the emphasis is on the effects of adolescent confusion and a solution is proffered. *Frühlings Erwachen* is a devastating exposé of the developing confusion of the adolescent mind as it struggles to come to terms with itself and with an adult world whose sole concern is self-interest and self-justification.

4

THE TRAGEDY OF ADOLESCENCE: *FRÜHLINGS ERWACHEN*[17]

Frühlings Erwachen, written between Autumn 1890 and Spring 1891, and based in some detail on Wedekind's personal experiences as a young man, also owes a strong debt to Büchner's play *Woyzeck*. Like Büchner, Wedekind is concerned less with individuals than with society as a whole, and he employs a loose associative technique in order to paint a picture of society rather than of any individual. The play consists of a series of unconnected scenes which follow each other in a sequence whose logic derives more from thematic progression and a pattern of cross-reference and contrast than a time sequence. Wedekind is very sparing in his indications as to when events take place. Though the play begins in the spring and ends on a clear November night, time and its passing are foreshortened so that the horrific nature of the events presented gain in effect. The economy of expression and the skilful manipulation and variation of mood heighten the tension and the growing sense of inevitable disaster.

This play does not depict the young set against the old in terms of the innocent against the guilty, nor does Wedekind see right exclusively on the side of youth. The fate of the younger generation obliged to come to terms with a stultifying bourgeois morality in order to survive also reflects the vicious circle of bourgeois life. How could their parents have developed any other than they did, and what standards other than those which they apply, can they, in

Wendla: Why did you make my dress so long, mother?
Frau Bergmann: You are fourteen now.
Wendla: I don't want to be fourteen if I have to wear a dress as long as that.
Frau Bergmann: It's not too long, Wendla. Whatever next! Can I help it, child, if you're two inches taller every spring? Now that you're growing up you can't go around in your princess dress any more.

(I,1; GW II, 97)

Wendla's question remains unanswered and her doubts and worries persist. In her innocence and ignorance she associates the dark thoughts that preoccupy her with this long dress that signifies 'growing up'. She draws a revealing contrast between such 'penitent's garb', as she calls her new dress (GW II, 97), and her favourite princess-style dress in which she can romp and indulge in fairy-tale fantasies. The gulf between reality and the way in which the adolescent mind interprets it is strikingly apparent. The insidious nature of what is being said is half concealed by the light tones of this short scene.

Wendla is not alone in her confusion. First the boys and then the girls are shown in contrasting variations on the same theme. The boys' search for some point to their existence is summed up by Moritz, who, as always, looks on the black side:

Why do we go to school? To be examined. And why are we examined? So they can fail us. They've got to fail seven of us anyway—there's only room for sixty in the next class. (I,2; GW II, 99–100)

The girls, too, equally at a loss to interpret adult behaviour, are already taking the first step towards conformity. Moritz and Melchior have had a lengthy and tortuous discussion on sex; the girls too reveal the hollowness of society. Their ignorance of the facts of life is compensated for by an emphasis on the outer face of family life: a crocodile of neatly turned-out children walking in line ahead of a proud mother. In its immediate context this is a refreshingly naive and touching scene, but the realisation that this is indeed the *reality* of the family life the girls will grow up to reveals the menace behind the enchanting picture.

The four opening scenes reveal a community of confusion and escapist fantasy which culminates in the first indication of the tragedy that will inevitably ensue. Act One closes with a meeting in the woods between Melchior and Wendla who is on her way home from taking food to the poor. At odds with himself and disgusted at the thoughts that Wendla's provocative beauty arouses in him, Melchior is all the more susceptible to the fantasy world in which she lives. Stifled by love, Wendla longs for 'reality'. She dreams of a wicked step-father who will beat her mercilessly, and entices Melchior to act out this rôle for her. The superior uncaring façade he has been at pains to project dissolves abjectly as Melchior whips Wendla across the legs as she demands, first gently then harder, and finally destroys the illusion by taking his fists to her. Overwhelmed by feelings he cannot control he rushes off in desperation. The victory of half-understood instincts over a rational pose prepares the way for the tragic developments of the second act.

Act Two opens and closes with Moritz Stiefel. The inner scenes of the act link his predicament to that of the other youngsters and make his suicide at the end of the act more than an isolated, if extreme, failure. Although Wedekind divided *Frühlings Erwachen* into acts, the action has a momentum which is maintained by a swift succession of scenes. This is crucial to the opening of the second act, for after Wendla's naturalness has reduced Melchior to a fair imitation of Moritz's despair at the end of Act One, Act Two opens with the two boys together, Melchior once more in control of himself, stressing his superiority to Moritz in school and in 'life' by smoking his cigarette in an adult manner and listening dispassionately while his friend pours out his heart.

The first three scenes of this act reveal varying reactions to the adolescent situation and with each one the noose tightens. Till now the older generation has been represented by a brief glimpse of the educational establishment and the fussing Frau Bergmann. Frau Gabor, Melchior's mother, appears to have the commonsense and liberal attitude that will redress the balance. She listens sympathetically to Moritz's troubles and on learning that he and Melchior have been reading Goethe's *Faust* suggests that they might have waited a little longer before studying that text since 'even the best can be harmful if you aren't old enough to understand it properly' (II,1; GW II, 123). However, Frau Gabor's reluctance to interfere with her son's activities, even though she recognises the harm they can do, is merely the other side of the coin to Frau Bergmann's evasions. Where Frau Bergmann treats her daughter as a child though she is fast growing up, Frau Gabor treats Melchior as the adult which the audience has just seen he is not:

> You are old enough, Melchior, to know what is good for you and what is not. Do whatever you feel is right. You know how proud and pleased I'll be if I never have to interfere. (GW II, 123)

Melchior cannot make that sort of judgement; Wedekind's technique of juxtaposition and montage in his scenes allows an unspoken irony to mar the benevolence of this scene. For all its liberal implications Frau Gabor's attitude is as evasive as Frau Bergmann's with which the audience is then presented in the famous 'facts of life' scene. 'Here I am', says Wendla to her mother's news of a new baby in the family, 'an aunt for the third time and

I haven't an inkling of how it all happens.' (II,2; GW II, 126–27) She has been fobbed off with the usual story of the stork, to which she delivers an implicit rebuke with a fairy-tale of her own. It has as much relevance and factual content as her mother's tale:

> *Frau Bergmann:* What are you doing? What are you staring at in the street?
> *Wendla:* A man, mother—three times as big as an ox. He's got feet like steamboats...!
> *Frau Bergmann (rushing to the window):* Rubbish! I don't believe it!
> *Wendla (quickly):* He's got a bedstead under his chin. He's playing 'Watch on the Rhine' on it. Oh! you've missed him. He's gone round the corner....
> *Frau Bergmann:* You and your stories! Giving your poor mother such a fright!
>
> (GW II, 126)

Frau Bergmann's attempt to enlighten her daughter, which leaves Wendla none the wiser, is presented in a manner that precisely illustrates the immature nature of their relationship, for Wendla kneels at her mother's feet and hides away from evil under her mother's apron in readiness for the worst. Frau Bergmann, though, has nothing to offer but the conventional fairy-tales and needs the security of an idyll to talk of the intimacies of reproduction. She sends Wendla off to see her sister, dressed in her princess dress like a lamb to the slaughter:

> May the good Lord bless you and keep you. When I've got a moment I'll sew a flounce on your dress. (GW II, 129)

This comforting picture is immediately shattered in a grotesque parody of the charade that Wendla and her mother have just enacted, which is at the same time an echo of Melchior's disgust at the sexual stirrings he cannot control. Hänschen Rilow locks himself in the lavatory to gloat over the latest of the voluptuous postcard reproductions of world art he has filched from his father's desk. The latest, and seventh, victim of this teenage 'Bluebeard' is Venus by Palma Vecchio. Hänschen longs for a breath of life, a touch of reality from these pictures; he can find neither relief nor pleasure that lasts. 'Venus' follows her six predecessors down the lavatory.

Hänschen's plea for a breath of life is answered immediately in the next scene. Wendla and Melchior meet in a hayloft while outside a storm is gathering. There is a parallel storm rising in the children too, but one they neither understand nor can master. Wendla's voice carries pathetically through the gloom in a grotesque misunderstanding of her mother's attempts to enlighten her:

Wendla: Don't kiss me, Melchior, don't kiss me.
Melchior: I can hear your heart beat.
Wendla: You love someone if you kiss them—no—no.
Melchior: There's no such thing as love!—It's all self and self-interest. I love you as little as you love me.
Wendla: No!—No! Melchior!
Melchior: Wendla!
Wendla: O Melchior!!—no—no—

(II,4; GW II, 132)

This encounter reverberates with echoes of what has gone before while at the same time carrying the action forward. There is no hint of the intercourse that will make Wendla pregnant. It is the logical progression from Hänschen's searching in the previous scene, and to dwell on what will happen is superfluous. In his search for an effective critique of society, Wedekind looks to motivation for and reactions to events rather than a presentation of the events themselves.

In complete contrast to the emotional turmoil of the hayloft, the scene that follows reveals Frau Gabor reading through a letter she has just finished. It is to Moritz who, having inevitably failed to make the grade at school, has made up his mind to run away. After the surging momentum which characterised the difficulties of the younger generation, the easy measured flow of Frau Gabor's reply spells out the gulf between the generations. The adult world finds Moritz's reactions incomprehensible, and by changing the mood and tempo in this scene Wedekind underlines the distance between the two worlds far more effectively than by a direct confrontation. Frau Gabor's expressions of sympathy glide benignly past the root cause of Moritz's dilemma, and her reaction to the moral blackmail she sees in his threat of suicide foreshadows the attitude she will later adopt towards her own son. Frau Gabor fulfils her social obligations to Moritz as she sees them—as a 'motherly friend' (II,5; GW II, 133), namely an adviser without responsibility. She cannot help Moritz and will prove equally at a loss with Melchior, and the swift succession of scenes ensures that the audience still has the vision of the hayloft in its mind. Frau Gabor lacks the emotional capacity for maternal responsibility and her measured rhetoric and liberal outlook conceal an inability to show and feel true sympathy.

The younger generation will be left to sink or swim on its own. 'If only someone would come along and I could throw myself in their arms and tell them everything!' (II,6; GW II, 134) This cry could have come from any of the adolescents; the words are in fact Wendla's as she is glimpsed in a brief poignant scene walking alone in the morning dew. The juxtaposition to Frau Gabor's monologue is a telling indictment of adult inadequacy.

Moritz too is desperate for such a confidant. He does not possess the energy to continue his losing battle with life and has taken himself down to the river and is ready to die. A confidant of sorts does come to Moritz, the nubile Ilse, but he is too full of inhibitions to cope with her freshness and *joie de vivre*. She seems to fulfil his worst fears about the overriding sexuality of life and he lets her go, burns his one last link to the world—Frau Gabor's letter—and as the flame flickers and dies his voice comes through the darkness and the sound of the water rushing by: 'It's dark now. I won't be going home any more.' (II,7; GW II, 142) Deliberately the act closes with an anticlimax. As with the scene in the hayloft, the event itself is incidental, so the suicide in all its messy detail is passed over till it can be used for greater effect in the reactions it arouses amongst the other children. (cf. III,2; GW II, 151)

Moritz's suicide is the fulcrum about which the third and final act revolves. When the essay Melchior wrote for his friend is discovered the adult world promptly casts him as scapegoat. Yet Moritz's predicament was not merely sexual, and here, by using a technique of cross-reference in his montage of scenes, Wedekind aims to emphasise the interaction of events. Moritz is primarily a social failure and it is both incidental that it was sexual awareness that helped drive him to collapse and also typical that society should seize on the symptom rather than the disease in order to exculpate itself. *Frühlings Erwachen* is not a tragedy of sex but the social tragedy of adolescence in which the emotional volatility of sex is the trip-wire; in order to stress this, the third act concentrates on the reaction of society to the events of the first two acts, and in so doing reveals the bankruptcy that will cause this situation to continue. The opening three scenes, in which the adults close ranks in self-defence, are presented with the full venom of Wedekind's skill as a caricaturist. It is an aggressive technique that forces the audience to face up to the author's accusations, while, through the medium of caricature, it is being shown the trap which society has sprung for its own members.

The act opens with the masters' meeting called to consider Melchior's position. The teachers are presented as narrow-minded cliché figures with surnames that sound like schoolboy nicknames—Sonnenstich (Sunstroke), Zungenschlag (Stutters), Fliegentod (Flycatcher), Knochenbruch (Fracture). Their unfeeling treatment of Melchior alienates the audience, an attitude it was half ready to adopt anyway, since schoolmasters hardly count as human beings in the first place. Wedekind encourages this attitude in order to turn it to his advantage. He equates the objectionable behaviour of the schoolmasters with the reaction of the rest of the community. The travesty in the schoolroom gives way to the grotesque pantomime of Moritz's funeral and is capped by the quarrel between Melchior's parents.

The masters' meeting has to be played as sixth-form end-of-term parody so that the audience reacts against what it sees. The caricatures are brutal; the meeting spends more time debating whether to open a window than it does over Melchior's case. The reason is simple. A decision on Melchior has already been made by the headmaster and the meeting is a formality to provide Rektor Sonnenstich with the rubber-stamp of collective responsibility for the action which is to be taken. Sonnenstich constantly reminds his colleagues of the collective nature of 'their' decision:

> We find ourselves faced with the necessary task of judging the guilty lest we, the innocent, are ourselves found wanting. (III,1; GW II, 145)

In this light, the puerile bickerings that counterpoint Sonnenstich's cliché-ridden monologue (for no-one is listening to him) emphasise the impotence of the cultural background. Fear and an awareness of their impotence reduce the masters to babbling incoherence; they too are conditioned to a norm of conformity and are unable to think other than in terms of the sake of appearances and the demands of society. In this respect Sonnenstich and Frau

Bergmann are alike. She turns to the abortionist to save Wendla's social position since she dare not assume the responsibility for enlightening her sexually. He will not accept responsibility for Melchior's moral position and searches desperately for a justification that will placate his critics, an insurance lest he be accused of professional incompetence. With a backward glance towards the Ministry of Education he decides that Melchior must go, lest they share guilt by association.

Fear, the motive force of so much of Wedekind's drama, provides a graphic illustration of the brutal trial of strength that society provokes. When Melchior, the 'enemy', appears, the masters compose themselves, put on their 'adult' faces and strike suitable poses so that the charade may begin. They become the dummies that Wedekind has drawn, for it is Sonnenstich who conducts the interrogation and he refuses to allow Melchior to deviate from a predetermined sequence of incriminating answers.

Behind Sonnenstich's verbiage and self-justification, Wedekind none the less implants the grain of truth that reflects Melchior's character. The boy has turned his essay for Moritz into a minor drama, a dialogue, and appears to have become so engrossed in what he was doing that he lost touch with the purpose of the exercise and has written to please and satisfy himself. After all, *twenty* pages of text with life-size illustrations was considerably more than would be needed to enlighten Moritz, who has no need of illustrations, having seen a naked woman at the local fair in Leilich's Anatomical Museum!! In his own way Melchior has echoed Frau Bergmann's fairy-tale of the stork. Unable to come to terms with unvarnished reality, as was apparent in his early discussions with Moritz (I,2 and II,1), Melchior has retouched it in response to his own needs. He is very much a part of this society that cannot say what it means except by circumlocution.

The implications of this scene extend to Moritz's funeral. The condolences the adults offer Moritz's father and each other are totally out of place:

> *Sonnenstich (shaking Herr Stiefel's hand):* It really was most improbable that we would have let him move up a class.
> *Knochenbruch (shaking Herr Stiefel's hand):* And if we had been able to let him move up, he was almost bound to have been kept down next spring.
>
> (III,2; GW II, 150)

Moritz's suicide is beyond the 'normal' pattern of behaviour; the apparent callousness of the teachers is really an attempt to conceal their sense of inadequacy by a retreat to the secure criteria of their profession. Even Moritz's schoolfellows fall back on a gruesome interest in detail in order to conceal their incomprehension at what he has done, while Moritz's father, who has no niche to escape to, makes a revealing comment on society's concept of parental responsibility: 'He was no son of mine.—He never gave me any pleasure from the start.' (GW II, 149) Only Pastor Kahlbauch (Baldbelly), who appears at the funeral in the security of his professional rôle, carries off the situation with aplomb. His measured, uninvolved tones reinforce the sense of outrage the adult world feels at Moritz's deed.

Melchior's expulsion is a direct threat to the social position of the Gabor household. Now that it is too late, Herr Gabor assumes responsibility for Melchior's education by sending him to a reformatory 'to develop a Christian way of thinking and feeling'. (III,3; GW II, 157). He announces his decision in a manner chillingly reminiscent of Sonnenstich's self-justifications, further illustrating society's prime concern with self-preservation:

> If we wish to keep a flicker of hope alive, and above all preserve a clear conscience as the parents of the boy, then it is

time for us to act with resolution and determination. (GW II, 154–55)

Frau Gabor's impassioned defence of Melchior which opens the scene coincides with the audience's interpretation of what it has just witnessed:

> They needed a scapegoat. They didn't dare let the accusations that were being made stick to them. And since my son had the misfortune to come along at the right moment am I, his own mother, expected to help these butchers. God preserve me from such a thought! (GW II, 153)

For a moment it seems parody is past and reality has at last been reached. Yet the reality of this deliberately humourless scene confirms rather than denies the trend of the previous two. Once again Wedekind cuts the ground from beneath his audience's feet. Frau Gabor's defence of her son appeals because it is what is expected of a mother, and by now the audience is ready to respond to any hint of naturalness, particularly when it hears Herr Gabor's string of platitudes. Frau Gabor's reaction is, however, one long cliché; it is pitched too high and reveals her playing out the rôle of devoted mother, the rôle she feels society expects of her and which she has fashioned and maintained to her own satisfaction over the years with Melchior's unwitting help.

When the second allegation, concerning Wendla—which is not yet public knowledge—is made, Frau Gabor can no longer sustain this rôle for she knows Melchior has turned away from her. Sympathetic understanding gives way to a concern for social appearances; her liberalism is exposed as a self-indulgent façade necessary for her own well-being. Frau Gabor is caught in a web of social behaviour in which personal feelings have given pride of place to external considerations. Despite herself she lacks the will and the strength to oppose her husband.

The three scenes that follow comprise a second assault on society's attitudes towards decency and obscenity. The reformatory to which Melchior is sent is presented with an explicitness that is deliberately shocking. The mood changes abruptly to lewdness and brutality as the audience is, quite literally, faced with a masturbation race played by the inmates. If these are 'degenerates' as the governor suggests, then the responsibility lies with a society which puts out of sight what it cannot cope with. Here (III,4), for the first time in this play, Wedekind is deliberately obscene in a direct challenge to the echo of Herr Gabor's Christian tenets. Significantly Melchior is depicted as an outsider in the institution; he cannot bring himself to join in, he has not yet been dragged down.

Melchior was sent to the reformatory by the Gabors' desire to pre-empt social blackmail, Wendla (III,5) is to be handed over to the abortionist because as the mother of an illegitimate child her social position would be intolerable. Frau Bergmann can think no further than that. Where Herr Gabor saw the reformatory as a place of Christian enlightenment she also turns to the Christian ethic in her desperate search for help. In an ironic echo of Pastor Kahlbauch's text at Moritz's funeral, she falls back on the maxim 'God helps those who help themselves':

> Let us put our trust in God, Wendla. Let us hope for His mercy and do what it is in our power to do. Nothing has happened *yet*, and if we don't lose heart then the good Lord will not desert us. Be brave Wendla, be brave. (III,5; GW II, 163)

This statement, frightening in its combination of a sincere desire to do the right thing for Wendla and its appeal to God as the higher instance who will approve the proposed action, reveals the dilemma of the individual brought up to respect the standards of society. It is all too easy to disparage Frau Bergmann, but society has so drained her of

THE TRAGEDY OF ADOLESCENCE

all self-reliance and so conditioned her that she truly believes she is acting in Wendla's best interests. Left alone, the audience learns later, Wendla would have given birth without difficulty. Stifled by an overprotective love that was unable to articulate the need for protection, she was a ready victim of the unnatural act which killed her.

But what constitutes an unnatural act? Again Wedekind's technique of scenic montage requires the audience to take stock. Compared to the barbarity that Wendla is about to undergo and the obscenity of the reformatory, the idyll on the hillside in the vineyard as Hänschen and Ernst confess their love for each other is a welcome breath of fresh air (III,6). Their love is as genuine as it will be shortlived. They will grow out of such homosexual by-play as they mature. Yet society is swift to disapprove of such relationships and even swifter to condemn their presentation on a stage. The natural beauty of this moment heightens the irony of the moralising condemnations it has aroused and makes Wedekind's point even more telling.

The final scene of the play is set in the cemetery where both Moritz and Wendla lie buried. It is now November. Melchior has escaped from the reformatory and is overwhelmed by Wendla's death for which he holds himself responsible. In his exhausted condition he is in no fit state to see beyond the barrage of fine words with which Moritz describes life beyond the grave and is sorely tempted to follow his friend's lead and commit suicide. Only the appearance of the mysterious 'masked gentleman' who puts Moritz in his place can guide him back towards life. Wedekind is quite specific as to why this ambiguous figure, to whom *Frühlings Erwachen* is dedicated, makes an appearance:

> I was reluctant to finish the play amongst the schoolchildren, without a glimpse of adult life. So in the last scene I introduced the masked gentleman. I chose the philosophy of

Nietzsche as the model for Moritz Stiefel rising from the grave, the embodiment of death. (GW IX, 424)[18]

However, the masked gentleman should not be equated with Wedekind himself, an error encouraged by the fact that Wedekind himself portrayed this rôle on stage, appearing after the audience had heard Moritz boasting glibly of the grandeur of life on his side of the grave: 'We take no notice of the comedian's mask, and we can see the writer putting on his mask in the darkness.' (III,7; GW II, 169)

The case for accepting the masked gentleman as the positive figure some critics have suggested is far from conclusive. While he certainly rescues Melchior from Moritz and death, the life offered by the masked gentleman has little to recommend it. The audience has just seen the reality behind Moritz's fine words and the masked gentleman puts nothing but equally fine-sounding words in their place. Melchior leaves for the adult world in the company of an individual whose most profound statement is that:

> One should never forget one's dignity. I define morality as the tangible product of two intangible quantities, namely inclination and obligation. Together they produce morality, and that's a fact of life. (GW II, 172–73)

There is very little difference between this and Melchior's own patronising statements to Moritz in the first two acts. Melchior began the play as a brash adolescent whose desire to patronise concealed a deep insecurity. The events of the play confirm that to survive in this society the individual must turn to the security of established, external, visible standards and Melchior's present situation stems from the fact that he allowed his natural instincts to fall foul of these standards. He has had no chance to learn of emotional, qualitative standards, so his life will indeed be one of 'enervating doubt' (GW II, 174) as the masked gentleman suggests. It is the latter's rôle to lead Melchior

THE TRAGEDY OF ADOLESCENCE

to life, and as such the dedication is sincerely meant, but when life appeared to Moritz as Ilse it was as overpowering sexuality, the Achilles' heel in Moritz's character; now, to Melchior too, life appears as an exaggerated form of his own failings. Under this tutelage and with the experiences Melchior has behind him, his view of life will, to say the least, be unbalanced. In assessing the force of the masked gentleman, it is not without significance that the play ends with Moritz settling back in his grave and musing over the immutability of life. Nothing has changed, nothing can change: 'The moon covers her face, unveils herself again, and doesn't look a scrap more intelligent.' (GW II, 174)

The question insistently posed throughout Wedekind's work is: how is it possible to pass through adolescence in such a society and yet emerge a normal balanced personality? While he offers no clear answer either way, the characters of *Frühlings Erwachen* share childhood experiences that are very similar to those which the characters in such plays as *Lulu, Franziska* and *Der Marquis von Keith* reveal that they have suffered too. The detailed analysis of adolescence in *Frühlings Erwachen* provides an insight into the adult world of Wedekind's social circus. *Frühlings Erwachen* is a tragedy of adolescence, but the tragic flaw in all Wedekind's characters is that they never grow up. Their emotional development is checked by their childhood experiences and bourgeois upbringing.

5

THE RISE AND FALL OF A
BEAUTIFUL DREAM: *LULU*

Wedekind struggled with the material of *Lulu* from 1892 until the summer of 1895 when he handed Albert Langen, his publisher, a completed manuscript, *Die Büchse der Pandora, eine Monstretragödie* (Pandora's Box, a Monster Tragedy). Langen saw probable legal repercussions in view of Lulu's death at the end of the play at the hands of Jack the Ripper and so Wedekind was obliged to divide up the five acts of his original scheme. The first published version of *Lulu* appeared as *Der Erdgeist* (The Earth Spirit) in 1895. This contained the first three acts of the Monster Tragedy with a new act inserted between Acts Two and Three. (The new Act Three is set in Lulu's dressing-room on the night of her début as a dancer.) The remainder of the original manuscript in a modified form was published in 1902 in the journal *Die Insel* prefaced by a new first act, in which everyone is waiting for Lulu to make her entry after her escape from prison. This gave the author a chance to place 'new readers' in the picture.

Erdgeist (as the first part became known) underwent little serious revision, but, as Langen had foreseen, legal reaction to *Die Büchse der Pandora* and Lulu's death resulted in drastic textual adaptation. Wedekind wrote various forewords and defences of the play but these should be treated with some scepticism, for their purpose was to win free passage for the work. Wedekind's forewords reflect the spirit of this comment on *Franziska*:

THE RISE AND FALL OF A BEAUTIFUL DREAM

> There is very little to say about *Franziska* on the theoretical side as yet, since I don't know how people are going to misunderstand the play. (GW IX, 453)

In particular Wedekind's claim that the real heroine is not Lulu but the lesbian Countess Geschwitz is specious. This is a deliberate attempt by the author to wrong-foot his antagonists, for while Geschwitz is undoubtedly the character who most closely approaches the requirements for that rôle in traditional terms, it is equally clear that Wedekind is not writing a traditional play. The central character is Lulu, everything revolves around her. The play is quite viable without Geschwitz who is but one of a number of variations on the central relationship, but without Lulu it would be a different play altogether.

Lulu is traditionally regarded as an embodiment of sexuality, of the emancipated flesh, an amoral physical force that acts instinctively and is incapable of rational thought. Critical attention has stressed her voracious sexual appetite and apparently indiscriminate destructiveness and Peter Barnes's adaptation follows this approach, tracing the sexual confrontations of a 'sex tragedy'. Wedekind, however, saw sex as an accurate barometer which revealed the extent of his characters' personal and social well-being. For him it is a *lingua franca* which everyone can follow—even though they may not fully understand what is being said—and it provides the one open channel of communication in a society trapped in the web of its own fear and insecurity.

The characters in *Lulu* do not listen to each other. They talk aloud for their own benefit, and their conversations are a juxtaposition of monologues. They talk past each other because they dare not talk directly to each other and risk a direct response to which they have no answer. The less than human impression conveyed as the exchanges fly incongruously between the characters is strongly reminiscent of the cross-talk and farcical exchanges that were such a feature of *Der Liebestrank*. This is reinforced by the speed and manner of their delivery which is deliberately tuned to the style of a vaudeville act. If it is difficult to take these characters seriously as human beings it is because in seeing them as inadequate Wedekind has chosen a manner of self-expression that will best illustrate their inadequacy. Lulu's is a world of egocentrics, each afraid to come to terms with the world as it is and each determined that the world of his imagination is a true reflection of the world outside. This pathological self-delusion is strikingly and comically illustrated in the different names Lulu acquires from her partners. Lulu ('quite antediluvian' is the comment of her 'father' Schigolch) is called Nelli by Dr. Goll who sees in her nothing more than a piece of baggage, referred to as Eva by the painter Schwarz who escapes from reality into an ideal world, and as Mignon by Dr. Schön, whose choice of a highly Romantic name for her betrays very early in the play the soft centre to the hard exterior he chooses to project. In stressing this essentially speculative aspect of human behaviour, Wedekind draws his characters larger than life, not because they are, but because they think they are. Inflation is the best way to prick the bubble.

The axis of *Erdgeist* and *Die Büchse der Pandora* is the relationship between Lulu and Dr. Schön. The rôle of the other characters is to modify and comment on the implications of this relationship, and to this end Wedekind uses the technique so successful in *Frühlings Erwachen*, namely juxtaposition and the use of recurrent and parallel situations. The plot in *Lulu* is, however, more explicitly traced.

The dilemma that faces Dr Schön as *Erdgeist* opens is one very common to Wedekind's characters: how to control a relationship which, begun under one set of rules, is

THE RISE AND FALL OF A BEAUTIFUL DREAM

rapidly acquiring a new and totally unacceptable structure. Schön's need for sexual indulgence without prejudice to his social position, that is, total personal freedom without limitations or responsibilities, has encouraged him to take advantage of the position of power he acquired when he caught the sixteen-year-old Lulu trying to pick his pocket. In *Pygmalion* fashion he took her in and educated her to fulfil a rôle that met his needs. He taught her to use her body to achieve social success. The audience hears of the start of this partnership from Lulu in Act Two when she is rejecting Schön's assessment of their relationship:

> When you caught me trying to steal your watch, what did you do? You took me by the hand and gave me something to eat and clothes to wear. Do you think I can forget that? Anyone else would have sent for the police. You sent me to school and taught me style. Who else in the world ever cared about me? I've danced and I've let myself be painted in oils and was content to keep myself that way. But I can't fall in love just because you say so! (II,3; GW III, 47)

Her words uncannily recall the situation of Melchior and the masked gentleman in *Frühlings Erwachen*. The echo does nothing to paint the masked gentleman in a more optimistic light.

Schön has cast himself as the man of iron, the unscrupulous manipulator and successful financier. His initial dominance over Lulu ensured that when his own bed-ridden wife died and there was no longer a chaperone in Schön's house, Schön could forestall social affront by marrying Lulu off to the elderly roué Dr. Goll. The choice of Dr. Goll as Lulu's first husband proves as ill-judged as that of Schwarz as her second, and for good reason. Schön dares not give Lulu to a man who might put his own prowess in the shade, and his initial collapse when Schwarz commits suicide in circumstances that will ruin Schön reveals that the true measure of Schön's success is as an illusionist. He is a caricature in the manner of George Grosz—a truly incongruous figure in society, but the fact is that the society which Wedekind portrays is *not* normal society. Schön is as much an outsider as was Schwigerling in *Der Liebestrank;* his two-year pursuit and eventual betrothal to Countess Adelaide von Zarnikow illustrates how keenly he feels the need to belong to the society he affects to despise, and whose morality he is so ready to disparage.

The conflict in *Lulu*, then, is less a battle between the sexes than a struggle by a series of individuals to survive in an environment hostile to their aspirations. It is not that sexual prowess guarantees success or sexual weakness indicates failure, but rather that sexual possession confers status by association. As the patron behind Lulu, Schön basks in reflected glory, provided that the devastating effect of her beauty can be directed elsewhere and harnessed, either by marriage to someone else, or in her artistic activities. Schön works towards his goal of social acceptance by means of his aristocratic fiancée, while reinforcing his image as a man who counts by acting as Lulu's protector. The inevitable conflict of interest that this situation provokes is beyond Schön's comprehension until it is too late. He has divided his life into self-contained compartments; viewed separately each can succeed, but when they inevitably clash Schön is lost. Sexual and financial equations are rife throughout the play, and indeed in a society as materialistic as Schön's it is hard to imagine things otherwise. The need for security introduces the morality of the stock-exchange into the world of emotional affairs and disaster inevitably ensues.

Dr. Goll's enjoyment of Lulu is that of an animal-trainer. She performs for him and dances to his tune, quite literally. There is no humanity to Goll, only an acute sense of self-preservation which Lulu vicariously keeps alive. He desires no children but uses her instead as a surrogate to fulfil his dreams of vigour. He represents a travesty of that side of Schön which seeks to make sexual and social capital out of possession of or involvement with Lulu. Goll is driven on by his sexual fantasies and finally destroyed by them. It is he who has commissioned the portrait of Lulu as pierrot, a picture that will follow her progress through both plays as a reminder of the past. He supervises its commission with scathing pedantry, transforming Lulu into a near mythical figure. His sexual appetite is aesthetic rather than physical, and his instructions to Schwarz are correspondingly precise:

> Her skin is pure white. I've never seen anything to match it. I've told our Raffael here to be as sparing as possible with the flesh colouring. I've no time for this modern smearing. (I,2; GW III, 19–20)

His desire for an essentially spiritual relationship is so at odds with Lulu's physical appearance that the incongruity of their match is underlined. Goll has one abiding fear: that Lulu will be unfaithful to him. His outward display of mastery is the product of an inner unease compounded by his own sexual impotence. It is fitting that his fatal heart-attack is provoked by the fear of a seduction that never took place. As the audience knows, Schwarz was too inhibited to finish what he began.

Where Goll represents a financial equivalent to Schön, Walter Schwarz reflects, in his career as an artist, Schön's innate vulnerability and escapism. He overcomes his inherent fear of Lulu by retreating into the inalienable world of his art, measuring the success of their marriage by the number of pictures she has inspired him to paint since their wedding-day. He has a romantic view of their relationship, and, until Schön is forced to reveal the truth, believes that he married a virgin. His abject collapse when the facts are laid before him foreshadows and parodies

Schön's own defeat. The irony of the confrontation between Schön and Schwarz in Act Two is that Schwarz's dreams and Schön's vision of Lulu are by no means so dissimilar. Neither of them regard her as anything more than a projection of their own fantasies. Schwarz's illusions lead to suicide and his suicide is only a step away from causing Schön's downfall. It takes the outbreak of revolution in Paris—a suitably unlikely *deus ex machina*—to extricate Schön.

As *Erdgeist* progresses the noose tightens round Dr. Schön. Act Three, perhaps because it was not part of the original *Lulu*, conveys a vivid impression of the stages in Lulu's progress, underlining the repetition and similarity of the fate that attends those men who are drawn to her:

> *Alwa Schön:* What a play I could write about her. Act One: Dr. Goll. Worm bait by now. I can quote Dr. Goll from purgatory or wherever he is paying for his orgies—they'll still blame *me* for his sins. . . . Act Two: Walter Schwarz. Even more incredible! Our souls are stripped bare in moments like these! Act Three?—Can it really go on like this?! (III,2; GW III, 65)

As a comparison of each death scene shows, it can.

As a parody and preface to Schön's attitude to Lulu, Wedekind introduces Prince Escerny, the latest consort chosen by Schön to keep Lulu at a safe but convenient distance. (The thought that Lulu might actually go back to Africa with Prince Escerny is a contributory factor to Schön's collapse in the face of Lulu's onslaught.) Escerny exercises a despotic rule over the natives in darkest Africa —an exotic equivalent to set against Schön's escapist illusions of power—and the prince's current desire to be dominated by a woman distorts Schön's position to reveal its essential truth. Escerny's fascination for Lulu's performance reflects her position as a catalyst. She inspires so many men because she can be all things to all men, for each can seek and find in her that which will accord with his own needs. As an artist on stage Lulu can bewitch, entrance and wreak havoc with her audience's responses and it in turn is free to respond because, having bought a ticket for her performance, it has set a clearly-defined limit to the confrontation. When the show is over the audience can go home.

What the public at large seek from their entertainment Schön practises in detail, attempting to translate the security of the performance into his own life. Lulu's giddiness when she sees Schön watching her with his fiancée at his side emphasises the security granted to her audience, while Schön's departure from the box in the auditorium to face Lulu in her dressing-room where he is no match for her, completes the equation. Lulu turns on him with the full intensity of her performance and at such close quarters he is powerless to resist her. Humiliated and broken he breaks off his engagement in words which Lulu dictates to him.

It is Lulu's misfortune that there is no-one who can help her to the self-fulfilment that she seeks. Thanks to Schön she has learnt to equate love with a struggle for mastery, and since her struggle has been with Schön she feels that he is the only one she has loved (cf. IV,8; GW III, 96). The pathos of her situation is that her efforts to experience 'love' —through the only common denominator, that of sex—only lead to destruction. She stands alone as the possessor of a natural vitality; those about her are not only unable to match it, but are destroyed by her misplaced efforts to establish a meaningful rapport.

Schön's marriage to Lulu spells the ruin of his dreams of greatness and hopes of a social position. Their relationship is deftly deflated by the Countess Geschwitz whose lesbian love for Lulu is as genuine as its chance of fulfilment is remote. In Geschwitz Wedekind caricatures the social relationships he portrays; the 'unnatural' lesbian has more 'natural' feelings than all the other characters put together (like the 'unnatural' relationship between Hans and Ernst in *Frühlings Erwachen*), but she is branded as different and society may thus ignore her. Schön's dream of a family home and of being part of society has similarly disappeared. His home is an asylum for the flotsam of society which Lulu attracts and his only escape is to the stock-market. There at least he still has the power and capacity to manipulate and control events and can measure his prowess in tangible terms.

The 'open house' he leaves behind him is a reminder of his real situation. Exaggerated language, grotesque characters and situations all provide routines straight from farce as Schigolch, the athlete Rodrigo, the truant schoolboy, the coachman Ferdinand and Alwa Schön vie for Lulu's attention. Instead of falling away when Schön unexpectedly returns to catch them *in flagrante delicto* the farce is heightened as characters disappear through windows, up chimneys and underneath tables with a facility totally at odds with the seriousness of the situation. For a moment it does seem that the blind passion and fury which burns in Schön will enable him to assert himself. He finds the strength to force Lulu to her knees with a revolver to her head, and for the first time she too breaks down. Her defence, born of desperation, none the less rings very true:

> You knew what you were doing when you married me—and I knew why I was marrying you. You'd deceived your best friends with me, you could hardly deceive yourself with me as well! You've given me your Indian Summer, but I've given you the full flower of my youth. You know ten times better than I do which is worth more. I've never set myself up to be *anything* that other people hadn't seen in me first—and they never took me for anything else but *me*. I know what you want. You'd like me to shoot myself. I may not be sixteen any more—but I'm still too young for *that*. (IV,8; GW III, 95)

THE RISE AND FALL OF A BEAUTIFUL DREAM

The irony is that Schön *has* deceived himself with Lulu and is now paying the price.

Wedekind introduces the alienating device of the grotesque to deny his characters the dignity they do not deserve. The climax of *Erdgeist*, Lulu's murder of Schön, is marked by a return to farce. Hugenberg pops his head out of his hiding place and momentarily distracts Schön. Lulu turns the revolver on Schön and empties it into him. It is a reflex action, an instinctive act of self-preservation, and it signs her own death warrant. Schön's death is the final travesty; there is no water to wet his lips, he must make do with champagne, the last vision he has before he dies is that of Geschwitz—a grotesque distortion of Schön's lust for sexual power—and the ending is counterpointed by Hugenberg's plaintive lament: 'I'll be expelled from school.' (GW III, 97). Where there is no humanity there can be no tragedy; the black comedy with which *Erdgeist* comes to a close reflects Wedekind's concern to illustrate the moral and emotional emptiness of this social circle.

Lulu is a predator because that was the rôle in which Schön coached her. She was taught to reflect the illusion required of her and this she has done. Since it transpires that the basis of her existence is reflected in her ability to fuse her personality into illusion, exemplified best in her dancing, it follows that when the image she is to reflect has vanished she will be helpless. Lulu's vulnerability at the end of *Erdgeist* indicts the materialistic approach society adopts to human relations, illustrated through the figure of Dr. Schön. Once Lulu is denied his protection and is alone, the vultures on the fringe of society can pick her clean.

Die Büchse der Pandora, which takes up the history of Lulu after her conviction and imprisonment for the murder of Dr. Schön, begins in marked contrast to *Erdgeist* with a long-winded and essentially static exposition. The Countess Geschwitz, Rodrigo and Alwa, gathered in what was Schön's house, recount the pre-history of the play, much of which is known to an audience which has seen *Erdgeist* and all of which is known to the three on stage. In addition to putting the audience in the picture, Wedekind's presentation serves also to emphasise how his characters ignore all considerations other than the rôle they themselves have played. In talking past each other the participants in this three-sided monologue underline the emptiness of their world and set the tone for what is to follow.

In general, the sense of desperate and frenetic activity that pulsed through *Erdgeist* has eased, yet the change in tone and pace reflects the new situation, for when the two plays are presented in one evening (as Wedekind originally intended his story to be told) the language and mood of *Die Büchse der Pandora* does not jar on that of *Erdgeist*. Dr. Schön's search for security and his relationship with Lulu provided a goal and an impetus; with his death the sense of purpose is missing. In addition, Lulu's trial and conviction have precluded all possibility of the social acceptance to which Schön aspired and which drove him to such extremes. There is now no need for the mask of pretension, the characters are outside society and realise this fact. They can no longer act, only react, and the hostile forces about them assume greater menace. Casti-Piani, the procurer who offers Lulu the choice between life in a luxury brothel in Cairo or recapture by the police, aptly illustrates her new vulnerability. If it was inevitable that Schön would destroy himself through Lulu, it is certain that without Schön Lulu will be plundered by those about her and, having lost the man she fought to possess, will lack the goal that sustained her and gave her such vitality in *Erdgeist*.

THE RISE AND FALL OF A BEAUTIFUL DREAM 93

Not that Lulu's friends have been idle. The lesbian Geschwitz has deliberately contracted cholera and is now about to complete her scheme to change places in prison with Lulu. It is a selfless act of love that is far-sighted enough to realise the obligation Lulu should feel towards her. Rodrigo has been making plans for the future; he will turn Lulu (now his fiancée) into a first-rate artiste so that he can retire on the profits of her exertions. Alwa, in the meanwhile, has immersed himself in literature. He is writing a new play, 'The Ruler of the World' (an echo of his father's inclinations), but is finding it hard work. Indeed, since his father's death, Alwa's writing has met with little response and he characteristically places the blame on the contemporary literary scene rather than on deficiencies in his own talents. Wedekind allows a mischievous note of farce to intrude into Alwa's lament; the comic effect helps deflate Alwa's posturing and seasons the jibe against the Naturalists:

> *Alwa:* That's what is wrong with literature today—it's too literary. We can't see any further than the end of our pen-nibs. We only write about the things that appeal to authors and academics. If we're going to put some life back into our art we must get out amongst people who have never read a book in their lives and who act out of sheer animal instinct. That was the principle behind my 'Earth Spirit'. I did my best. The woman I based it on has spent the last year behind bars and I can only get the play performed in theatre clubs. I don't understand it. While my father was alive I could get my work performed anywhere in Germany. Things have taken a turn for the worse. (I; GW III, 125–26)

The irony to which Wedekind is working here and in Alwa's reaction to the young Alfred Hugenberg, who also steps out of the past for a moment, is that Alwa's disparagements of his colleagues are equally apt for himself. 'The Ruler of the World' will take life and turn Hugenberg into art, just as Alwa has described his 'Earth Spirit'.

He is the eternal parasite who can only sustain himself by translating his problems into art:

> *Alwa:* My sensuality and creative urges have the closest affinity. When I think of you I have a simple choice: to write a play about you or make love to you.
> *Lulu (as if telling a fairy-tale):* At one time I dreamt for nights on end that I'd fallen into the hands of a sex-murderer. Come on, give me a kiss.
>
> (GW III, 142)

Lulu's apparently irrelevant reply, prophetic in itself, also provides the key to the eventual appearance of Jack the Ripper. Like Alwa and the other men in her life, he preys on Lulu as a means of sustaining an otherwise seemingly normal life. The audience may regard his relationship with Lulu as a grotesque travesty, but it is in fact a clear indictment of society's own perverted morality. Jack's shadow falling across Lulu at this early stage of *Die Büchse der Pandora* emphasises how much the hunter has become the hunted. The dark comedy of this first act with so many faces and echoes from the past only stresses how much Lulu is now a helpless prisoner of events in a downward spiral.

Act Two, set in an opulent private gaming-room in Paris about a year after Lulu has made her escape from prison, illustrates the false glitter of Lulu's new way of life. She survives, thanks to her lack of emotional feeling and her sense of self-preservation, but the veneer of respectability which cloaked such activities in *Erdgeist* has been stripped away. This is the function of *Die Büchse der Pandora*. It is not merely the telling of Lulu's fate to its conclusion, but an exposure in clear-cut terms of the mechanism that leads to that fate. Lulu acts no differently now than in *Erdgeist* and the same may be said of those about her. The difference is the absence of a sense of conventional behaviour which acts as society's moral fig-leaf. The open sexual and financial speculation of this act pillories the covert dealings of *Erdgeist*. Again, in keeping with the subhuman level of society, the manner of speculation is presented in comic terms. In addition to his activity at the gaming-table the banker Puntschu has been doing a brisk trade in 'Jungfrauaktien' (literally 'Virgin shares'; these are shares in a scheme to build a railway to the summit of the Jungfrau mountain in Switzerland). The opportunities for double entendres are not missed and the implicit sexual prowling of Schön's society is exposed through the interest expressed in the twelve-year-old daughter of one of the guests at the gaming session. To survive Lulu must exploit those weaker than herself and, lacking the money to buy security, turns to Geschwitz whose emotional dependence makes her vulnerable. There is no more graphic illustration of the emotional sterility in this society than Lulu's exploitation of the countess; the effect of her demands on the unfortunate countess would be truly tragic if Wedekind did not ensure that his audience could not take this world seriously.

The animal cruelty of Lulu's schemes is presented in a sequence of melodrama, comedy and farce. The 'Virgin shares' collapse and the outlook is correspondingly bleak for the twelve-year-old virgin; Banker Puntschu accepts the situation with a fatalism that is hardly surprising. He prepares to start again for the thirty-sixth time. Lulu has no means of buying off Casti-Piani and has no intention of taking up his offer of luxurious exile; she escapes by changing clothes with the lift-boy. The police make a dramatic, but mistaken arrest. The whole of the second act has shown Lulu in a world that parodies her erstwhile luxury. The figures of Casti-Piani and Puntschu, an unsuccessful version of Dr. Schön, reduce the elegance of the setting to its tawdry reality.

The final act of *Die Büchse der Pandora* takes place in a

garret in London, where Lulu is about to make a new début: this time as a common street prostitute. Throughout the act Alwa, full of self-pity for himself, indulges in long, rambling reminiscences which recapitulate the glory that is gone, and through these Wedekind emphasises the contrasts (and the basic similarities) between then and now. Throughout both plays Lulu has vehemently rejected any suggestion that she could sell herself for money; now that she is shorn of all protection, society exacts its final revenge for her earlier success. Wedekind indicts the society that would condemn Lulu as a whore by showing how little she is suited to that profession. Like Melchior in the reformatory in *Frühlings Erwachen*, Lulu is totally out of place in her new rôle. As a prostitute she should find a financial and sexual security in her dealings which she has not known since Schön's death, but she attracts as weird a collection of misfits and inadequates in her new career as she had in her more elegant days. The arrival of Geschwitz with Schwarz's portrait of Lulu as a pierrot adds the final ironic touch.

There is no real difference between the two sets of men who have been drawn to Lulu under the spell of this portrait; the magnetism that radiates from the painting and recalls her triumphs is paralleled by the function she performs for her new clients. Both sets have needed her for their own sakes, the latter group, including as it does a mute, an African prince, a virgin academic who needs experience before marriage, and finally Jack the Ripper, is an explicit comment on the true face of the society in which Lulu has moved. In its final moments *Die Büchse der Pandora* reveals the stunted, twisted motivations behind the glitter of social life.

The Lulu plays focus on the fringe of respectable society and are exclusively peopled by individuals who do not belong to respectable society. The plays are thus hermeti-

I'm thinking seriously of building myself a house. A house with enormous rooms, a park, a sweep of steps curving up to the front door. And clumps of beggars, don't forget the beggars, in decorative clusters on the drive. I've broken with my past and good riddance! (I; GW IV, 12)

His essentially bourgeois aspirations, neatly exposed in this daydream, constitute the flaw in Keith's character. Try as he may, Keith cannot be the adventurer he pretends to be; the strain of keeping up with his own dreams proves too great.

König Nicolo has an historical setting. Nicolo, the fifteenth-century ruler of Umbria, has taken advantage of his position to live a life of sexual excess and self-indulgence, appearing to his subjects only at Carnival time, and even then masked. His middle-class citizens, outraged at his bad example and unwilling to put up with a king who is unable to do his 'job' properly, rise up against him, send him into exile and, in an ironic echo of the situation in Act Five of *Der Marquis von Keith*, put one of their number, master-butcher Pietro, on the throne in his place. Now that it is too late, Nicolo finds that, despite the sentence of death that hangs over him if discovered, he cannot tear himself away from his native country to live in exile. He seeks in vain to make his way as one of the people, but try as he may, he finds it impossible to deny his origins. Only as an artist on the stage, as a king in a royal farce, can Nicolo find some solace and acceptance by society.

The price Nicolo pays for his earlier self-assertiveness is characteristic of that paid by all such characters in Wedekind's plays. He is listened to, admired and applauded, but kept at arm's length. For all his efforts he can never be a full member of society. Nicolo's final position as court jester to his usurper gives him a fool's licence; he may dazzle with verbal wit, impress with force of argument and offer comfort to King Pietro in times of stress. He can project himself as the ideal king he would have liked to be, and which, given a second chance, he could be in practice; he will never be called upon, though, to live up to his fine words. Nicolo has achieved a position that would be the envy of characters such as Schön, Gerardo, Keith and Buridan, and Wedekind shows its basic weakness. Society condemns Nicolo to live a life without meaning, full of continual humiliation. His former life—which is representative of that of the artist-figure in Wedekind's plays—has been institutionalised and stands revealed as the hollow sham it was.

The Marquis von Keith has plans to give Munich a vast entertainment complex, the 'Feenpalast' (literally 'Fairy Palace')[21] with himself as its director and uncrowned king. He is hard at work drumming up support for this 'Magidome' amongst those of the outer circle in Munich society whose social aspirations make them less careful about where they put their money than they would otherwise be. The story of *Der Marquis von Keith* follows Keith's plans to within a hairsbreadth of success and documents a catastrophic defection of the support he painstakingly engineered. Keith finds himself outsmarted by the very society he had thought to exploit and has to see his brainchild prosper without him.

Wedekind's technique of variation and comparison is continued in this play by surrounding Keith with companions who in their different ways comment on the motivation and potential of his attitude. In addition to Molly Griesinger who is a constant reminder to him of past failures, Keith has in Anna Werdenfels, a voluptuous beauty of thirty, what he himself refers to as his 'living, breathing good-luck charm', (I; GW IV, 9). Anna is 'the other woman' in his life, the fulfilment of every Walter Mitty's aspirations. A more direct counterpart to Keith is provided by Ernst Scholz. He and Keith were brought up together on Scholz's family estate where Keith's father was tutor. Their shared upbringing has sent both of them off at a tangent to normal development, and after a life of failures Scholz has come to Keith for lessons in how to enjoy life.[22] Wedekind describes their relationship as 'the interplay between a Don Quixote of pleasure (Keith) and a Don Quixote of morality (Scholz). Keith tries to usurp morality as a means to his end, Scholz pleasure as a means to his. (GW IX, 429) Neither can help tilting at windmills and neither has the inner mental equilibrium to see things as they really are. Set against Keith is the figure of Consul Casimir, the leading light of the Munich business world, who remains unmoved by Keith's scheme to the point at which his opposition threatens to extend to those backers Keith has found. In his desire to reassure them, Keith forges a telegram in Casimir's name. All Casimir needs to do after that is bide his time; when he is ready he can sweep Keith aside as a proven criminal, move in and take over.

Though *Der Marquis von Keith* has the appearance of a 'well-made play' Wedekind's own analysis of the play shows how much it has in common with the 'station drama', in which emphasis is laid on a montage of significant events and situations rather than a closely-worked development of the plot, and how concerned he was to indicate parallels and comparisons:

Act One: Keith and Scholz are in dire straits.
Act Two: Keith and Scholz find new hope.
Act Three: Both are in their seventh heaven. Their Achilles heel is clearly visible.
Act Four: Scholz tries to play the schoolmaster and lecture Keith. Both their worlds collapse about them.
Act Five: 1. Keith's business enterprise deserts him.
2. His companion in luxury deserts him.

3. His companion in misery deserts him.
4. His companion for life deserts him.

(GW IX, 429–30)

Der Marquis von Keith is a play about a business enterprise built on an illusion. Keith has no money of his own, and, lacking funds, can only deal in words. The absence of business detail from the play is in keeping with Keith's character: he is no businessman—he does not keep books or accounts. Keith designs grand schemes and leaves it to others to fill in the details and pay the rates.

Keith is a clear-cut example of Wedekind's use of dialogue in characterisation. As he does, so he speaks. His *bon mots* and epithets and the impressive quality of his aphoristic *tours de force* give his views and position at first sight an almost impregnable authority. The throw-away lines, *non sequiturs* and verbose grandiose allusions of the masked gentleman in *Frühlings Erwachen* or of characters in *Lulu* which reflected the lack of communication in those plays are refined here into a more polished performance. The essence of an aphorism is that it is a pithy statement, a telling debating-point, a piece of verbal conceit and a stroke of brilliance that pre-empts response, and this is the means of Keith's precarious survival. He is preoccupied with the need to keep one move ahead, but his constant efforts to maintain this lead disturb rather than reassure those he is trying to impress. In addition the fluency of his dialogue is undermined by his physical appearance, always a prime consideration in the world Wedekind depicts.

Keith is almost perfect, but not quite, the flaw is evident from the start. In the opening stage-direction Keith is introduced in these terms:

He is about twenty-seven years old: medium height, slim, bony physique. His figure would be perfect if it were not for a limp in his left leg. His features are vigorous and alert, at the same time rather hard. . . . He is exquisitely but not foppishly dressed in a finely tailored suit. He has the coarse red hands of a clown. (I; GW IV, 5)

Keith's limp is unmistakable, his coarse hands belie the studied elegance of the figure he cuts. Wedekind gives his characters the dialogue in which they can inflate their egos, but ensures that their movements and gestures provide an unspoken comment to the audience. In a society that judges by external appearances because it lacks the capacity to look for intangible values, the restless jerkiness of Keith's movements is a fearsome handicap, and Wedekind underlines the ambiguity of Keith's position in the opening moments of the play.

The curtain rises on what appears to be a scene of typical bourgeois domesticity. Keith, at work in his studio, is brought a tray of refreshments by his wife:

Molly: Here we are, darling. Tea, cold meat and caviare. It was nine o'clock when you got up today.
Keith (without moving): Thank you, sweetheart.
Molly: You must be starving. Have you heard then? Are you going to get your Wonder Palace?

(GW IV, 5)

The real state of affairs swiftly emerges from the tone and nature of their exchanges, but, as happened to Schwigerling in *Der Liebestrank*, Wedekind has placed Keith where he really belongs before the adventurer himself has a chance to present his version. All that Keith says and does is set against this first impression. Keith is a bourgeois at heart but cannot admit it to himself. The tensions this cause lead directly to his persistent lack of success.

Whatever impelled Keith, who is some ten years older than Molly, to take her with him, two years in her company have taught him that she cannot shed her bourgeois ways and is a liability both to the image he projects to the world and the interpretation he places on his own rôle. Far from remaining the star-struck adolescent whose naiveté and dreams of adventure allowed Keith to play the man of the world to her when they first met in Bückeburg, Molly has developed into a clear-sighted observer and commentator on the fruitlessness of his efforts.

Molly shares Keith's inner turmoil, she is torn between her bourgeois background which is too strong for her to deny and her love for Keith, which he is unable to return to her in kind. She passes for Keith's wife, though she is not:

> Lord knows I don't want to name names. But all over the world—no matter where—if you want to get married you've got to have papers. And that's beneath his dignity—having papers. (II; GW IV, 35)

Both she and Keith know that if he is successful he will leave her and that while he is not, he still needs her. In her confused emotional state Molly finally begins to believe that this time Keith will succeed. The prospect of life without the man she loves is too much; the strain of their way of life has warped her otherwise clear judgement and she drowns herself. Ironically, the scandal this act will arouse is the surest means of guaranteeing that Keith will fail. Were he the man of steel he pretends to be he would have rid himself of Molly long ago and would be safe from such considerations as the weight of public opinion, but he cannot. He even admits to a sense of responsibility for her—surely the height of bourgeois respectability. A sentimentalist despite himself, Keith's relationship with Molly underlines his very real lack of inner self-confidence.

The bourgeois world is a world of property, the *sine qua non* of success. Keith cuts short the idealistic notions of the fifteen-year-old Hermann Casimir (Consul Casimir's son) who rejects money for the higher things in life:

These things are only called higher because they grow out of money and are only possible with money. Your father's made a fortune, so you're free to be a Rembrandt or a Darwin—as you like. But if you overlook the basic principle—money is freedom—you're asking the confidence men to take you over. (I; GW IV, 8)

Keith lacks such a financial base, and his position outside society obliges him to reverse this principle and, by spectacular involvement in his artistic venture, hope to convince those within society that since he occupies such an elevated position he must have the means to justify it. This is a brilliant ploy for as long as it succeeds, but Keith has prophesied his own fate, with the ironic twist that the confidence men who take *him* over are respected pillars of Munich society. The difficulty lies in deciding who the real confidence tricksters are. The whole world of *Der Marquis von Keith* is a masquerade, with characters appearing under assumed names at every turn. Keith greets Ernst Scholz, alias Count Trautenau as 'Gaston'; Countess Werdenfels is identified to Consul Casimir by Inspector Raspe (who himself used a French name in his murky past) as the ex-shopgirl Anna Huber from the Perusastrasse; Keith has rechristened his servants Joey and Katie Sascha and Simba respectively, and he has not forgotten his own cover-story:

I've as much right to be Marquis von Keith as you have to be Ernst Scholz. I'm the adopted son of the Lord Keith who in 1863 . . . (II; GW IV, 31)

It is not what you are, it is what you can get away with that counts in this society.

Since Keith is trying to get into society through the back door by using others' efforts, his choice of Art as his means to this end is apt. He also has the body of the beautiful Anna Werdenfels at his disposal and may exploit her beauty as Schön did with Lulu. In Anna Keith sees the embodiment of all his dreams, yet she is even more representative of them than he realises. She has made the transition which eludes Keith. Her beauty (an equivalent currency to wealth) enabled her to marry the Count, her late husband, and acquire a sound social position. She has learnt from experience that emotion is a dispensable luxury, and this matter-of-factness, which makes her so attractive to Keith, will also prove his undoing. When Anna sees which way the wind is blowing, she is swift to throw in her lot with Keith's arch-rival Casimir and bring *him* the security of reflected glory that Keith thought to make his own. While Keith imagines that he is exploiting Anna it is she who is using him. His brilliance makes her fortune, and she has the good sense to quit while she is ahead. She is all Keith would be, and all he will never achieve; she uses her bourgeois background to keep her feet on the ground, she never allows herself to be carried away by wishful thinking and, consequently, she emerges as the speculator who succeeds.

Anna is Keith's trump card in his scheme to use the Magidome Art Palace to establish himself in society. Indeed she is the only card he has to play, and this he does at a gala concert to launch the project. Keith designs Anna a dress for her début on the concert platform in which, he assures her, she will be a success even if she sang like a corncrake. In keeping with his sense for external appearances as a reflection of inner qualities, the dress is moulded to Anna's body as if it were a second skin, and Keith describes it to her in loving detail:

> A shimmering cascade of sea-green silk with sequins from shoulder to ankle, close-fitting, cut low back and front, encasing your slender body in a glittering sheath. (II; **GW IV** 46)

Keith's prediction is correct, but his skill as an illusionist proves to be to his own disadvantage. Consul Casimir, who has pointedly held aloof from Keith's scheme, pays his respects to Anna on the morning after her début and congratulates her on her performance:

> *Casimir:* I must compliment you on the choice of your concert-gown last night. You carried yourself with such—bravura—that, I admit, I could hardly follow your song recital with the concentration it deserved.
> *Anna:* Please don't think I overestimate my artistic talent.
> (IV; GW IV, 70)

The irony of Keith's deviousness is continued in Act Five with the first step towards Keith's ultimate isolation. Councillor Ostermeier, one of Keith's backers, becomes suspicious enough of Keith's dealings to demand to see account books which do not exist. Keith throws his notebook on to the table in front of Ostermeier with a lofty gesture that conceals his desperation. Ostermeier picks it up and reads where it has fallen open—a well-thumbed page: ' "A shimmering cascade of sea-green silk with sequins from shoulder to ankle." That just about sums you up!' (V; GW IV, 86) Ostermeier is well enough aware of Keith's tactics with Anna to recognise the same in his financial dealings. In this field too Keith is destroyed by the means of his success. Ostermeier and his cronies who have the resources to show if their bluff is called, can call Keith's bluff now and take him over.

The principal counterpart to Keith is his childhood companion Ernst Scholz. Scholz too feels outside society and longs to gain admittance as a useful member of society, an *idée fixe* that is his sole motivation. He is a mirror-image of Keith, he shares the same past, a similar history of repeated personal failure, and he too unsuccessfully tries to woo Anna, but to become his mistress. In all that he does he distorts and twists some trait of Keith's character and thus reveals the latter's equally grotesque psychological inadequacies. Scholz is there to be laughed at, but through him the true pathos of Keith's hotheaded activities is apparent.

Scholz's purgatory began with a railway accident, caused when he altered a railway regulation. As a consequence 'nine men, three women and two children died'. (I; GW IV, 22) Determined to purge himself by self-sacrifice Scholz comes to Keith to be guided to a life of total pleasure. He has tried hard work and total dedication without success, now he feels he must lose himself in the only logical alternative. Scholz feels that his wealth stands in his way—a view Keith dismisses as blasphemy, but it is Scholz's money which gives Keith a first foothold and it is the promise of more which keeps his hopes alive. Scholz spends the play battling towards a sense of self-confidence. Ironically, when he thinks he has found it, he expresses his self-possession by increasing the number of people who died in 'his' railway accident from fourteen to twenty. (IV; GW IV, 73) Now that he feels a new man, he can take more upon himself. His world crashes as inevitably as will Keith's and, faced with the realisation that he cannot hope to come to terms with this society, Scholz decides to retreat to an asylum where he will be able to refashion the world to suit his own needs without opposition. He would rather lose his reason than accept that he is excluded from life. Keith's desperate search for security drives him to turn his back on personal relations rather than acknowledge that his place is outside society.

Scholz and Keith clash for the last time towards the end of Act Five. Scholz's decision to enter the asylum and his wish to take Keith with him is presented in a grotesque mock auction. Scholz has promised Keith 20,000 marks and has advanced him 10,000 already. As Keith sees this loan slipping away from him and realises how close he is to the edge of a precipice he, like Scholz before him, expresses his desperation in the only terms that have real meaning. Scholz was burdened by the load on his conscience, Keith is concerned with his bank balance. The more Scholz refuses to help Keith, the greater the latter's desperation, which he expresses by raising the original 20,000 mark loan in stages to 40,000. There is no more natural way for Wedekind to present Keith's despair than in terms of hard cash.

Scholz's departure is followed by the arrival of the patrons from the Hofbräuhaus with Molly's corpse, fished out of the water where it has been for a week. Keith is saved from lynching by the arrival of Consul Casimir who drives them out and then buys Keith's immediate departure from Munich with a cheque for 10,000 marks (the sum Scholz originally offered Keith): 'Received from me . . . owed to you by Countess Werdenfels.' (V; GW IV, 98) It would seem that Anna Werdenfels has started as she means to go on. There was no mention of such a debt in the play.

Left alone with Molly's corpse Keith weighs up his situation: suicide or a new start with 10,000 marks? Given the shallowness of Keith's character there is only one decision, he puts down his revolver and with a wry shrug of the shoulders sets out to start again somewhere else. The shock and unexpectedly brutal ending to *Der Marquis von Keith* reduces life to the morality of a bowling-alley. It is directed against the materialist society that has outmanoeuvred Keith and bought him off. Keith survives to indulge in another speculative venture, with a far greater security than he has ever known. With 10,000 marks in hard cash, more than he has ever had of his own before, he should be able to transform failure into success and build himself his dream house.

The true satire of the play is at the expense of a bourgeoisie that rewards those who speculate on its own weaknesses. *Der Marquis von Keith* condemns not just Keith's emptiness, but, through the fates and actions of those he encounters, the social sphere in which he moves. This, because it is motivated by the same considerations as the society of the day and of the audience, includes the world at large.

Wedekind's bitter disappointment at the reception given to *Der Marquis von Keith* spurred him on to a retort with *König Nicolo*. Laced with allusions to Wedekind's own recent trial for *lèse-majesté* and to his fate as a writer whom the public did not take seriously, *König Nicolo* is not a confessional drama but shows that Wedekind is artist enough to put his own situation to effective dramatic use. While King Nicolo is clearly of a higher intellect than either his subjects or his worthy, but rather pedestrian successor, King Pietro, his fate is shown to be entirely of his own making. Nicolo has failed to put his personal talents to good use and society as a whole is the poorer for it. Wedekind condemns society for its preoccupation with the second-rate, but holds Nicolo equally to blame for not living up to his own social obligations.

König Nicolo is the sombre counterpart to the comedy of *Der Marquis von Keith*. The play follows the discoveries Nicolo makes about himself, and then shows how these confirm even more his lack of harmony with society. If Keith was the outsider in his society because he lacked the material foundations to underpin his schemes, Nicolo is the outsider here by virtue of the quality of mind and dignity associated with kingship. As his character develops it is clear that his future is his past. He only learns how to act and think as a king should when his earlier excesses have destroyed his daughter's chances of happiness. Wedekind's characters long to be able to start again; this chance is given to Nicolo who has officially been declared dead presumed drowned, but he is no more able to escape from himself than were his counterparts in the other plays.

PALACES AND KINGS 111

The clear perspective that the conventions and trappings of an historical setting allow lends the play a steadier pace. The Marquis von Keith was fighting an amorphous barrier that could be raised by sheer verbal fluency, but the forces which hold King Nicolo back are clear for all to see, and obviate the necessity for quick-fire exchanges and allow a more measured progression. Nicolo's inability to leave his native Umbria is representative of the fate that dogs most of Wedekind's characters: namely, their inability to deny their origins completely. They are all prisoners of their own past. What had been allusion in *Der Marquis von Keith* is made explicit in *König Nicolo* and this may well explain the readier audience appreciation of this play. Even though Wedekind has noticeably changed key, his theme is still the same.

In its structure too, *König Nicolo* is more clear-cut. Concentration on the crucial moment or breaking-point as an episode in a psychological adventure is the backbone of Wedekind's technique; in this play the lapses of time between 'stepping-stones' are easier to accept. Nicolo's progress to self-discovery—the ultimate goal of all Wedekind's work—is more drawn out than Keith's swift rise and fall and less elliptical than the path which *Lulu* trod.

The play has three acts, each subdivided into 'Bilder' (independent scenes). As Nicolo makes his voyage round himself, these 'Bilder' reinforce the essentially internal nature of the struggle. Act One has four scenes: the revolt and Nicolo's banishment; Nicolo as a beggar on the byways of his own land; Nicolo as a tailor's apprentice accepted back into society under an alias; Nicolo's trial and second banishment for *lèse-majesté*. Act Two has three scenes, tracing Nicolo's life in the social wilderness: as a prisoner in gaol; with his daughter on their way to join the travelling folk at their annual gathering under the gallows; at the gathering of outcasts where Nicolo's 'tragical performance' of his life history is hailed as high comedy and leads to his employment as a comic actor. Act Three has only two scenes. These reflect the extent of Nicolo's rehabilitation in society: now the stars of a travelling troupe of actors, Nicolo and his daughter Alma give a command performance of their royal farce which the audience (with the exception of King Pietro) find vastly amusing; Pietro, impressed by Nicolo's wisdom and outraged by the lack of understanding his subjects show, takes Nicolo from public view and installs him as his court jester.

The society that rejected Nicolo as its king when all he did was to play the fool now applauds his true wisdom as farce. Only Pietro is able to sense the validity of what Nicolo says and even he draws a clear line of demarcation beyond which Nicolo may not step. The mutual understanding between outsider and society which is illustrated through the bond between Nicolo and Pietro is controlled by the latter. Thus, when a love relationship threatens to develop between Alma and Pietro's son Filipo, Pietro demands that Nicolo put an end to it. Nicolo confesses to his true identity in the hope of rescuing his daughter's happiness—and is obliged to realise that while they will all listen to the wisdom of his foolery, no-one can afford to take him seriously. He dies in frustrated despair, whereupon society is prepared to believe his story. Alma and Filipo may marry, Nicolo is to be buried in the royal crypt but no-one must learn who he was. Society closes its ranks against all intruders until they are no longer a threat.

The tragedy of *König Nicolo* is that of a man who attempts to replace reality by dreams and who is deceived by the trappings of art—mask and costume—into believing that he has given his dreams a concrete basis. Nicolo fails as a king except in his rôle as king in the royal farce. Even there, though Nicolo presents King Pietro with the image of the king he would like to be, Nicolo's act is wishful thinking. The more practical Pietro is well aware that it is not always so easy to find honest and clever statesmen to replace the corrupt ones. In his mind and in his art Nicolo has resolved the problems that defeated him in life.

Nicolo fails by the standards of bourgeois practice too, since he can neither protect Alma during his lifetime nor provide for her after his death. In fact she adapts to her new life far better than he does, and finds her own future happiness; here too Nicolo proves an irrelevancy. His reaction to these continued failures shows how much he wishes to belong to society and how it is his own character which defeats him. As the tailor's apprentice in the first act he caught his master's eye by the skill with which he could design and cut fine gowns for the ladies, but undid this good impression because he was unable to sew the pieces together so that they would not come apart in the middle of the dance. This episode graphically illustrates the ambiguity of Nicolo's situation. To quote the Marquis von Keith, he has sold his birthright for a mess of pottage. Wedekind's choice of the figure of a king as a fulcrum for this drama embraces the combination of personal, psychological and social forces which have conspired against the characters in his other plays. Such *is* the life that Wedekind's characters are forced to lead.

König Nicolo is prefaced by a Prologue which, in Brechtian fashion, directs the audience to seek the cause rather than contemplate the symptoms. Dressed as court jester and bajazzo respectively, Nicolo and Alma step before the curtain for Nicolo to open the play with the words:

No laughter, please! You are fools too. As blind as I am. (GW IV, 105)

This explicit identification of stage with auditorium in a common failing is intended to encourage the audience to forget its escapist reasons for coming to the theatre and learn to recognise itself in the action on the stage. In each of us, the dialogue between father and daughter continues, there lurks a petty king and a great fool. In our own way we are all Nicolos. The audience that sees the events that follow not as costume drama but as an illustration of a universal human condition will, says Nicolo, truly be the witness of a royal performance for it will have shown regal intelligence. Alma is concerned with the fool searching for the land of his childhood dreams and ignoring everything else in his desperate quest. No matter what he does there is only one unforgivable crime: to forget that you are a human being and the dignity that goes with that. This is the theme of *König Nicolo*; the gloss and colour of the costume trappings should not blind the audience to the basic struggle to retain one's dignity in a hostile environment.

The concepts of human dignity and personal majesty opposed to the escapism of illusion and fairy-tale are the pivots around which the plot of *König Nicolo* revolves. As the play proper opens and the audience meet the fool and bajazzo as king and princess, the ironic detachment which Wedekind sought to arouse in his audience begins to work. The evening's performance begins with Nicolo in the rôle in which he ends the play. The hindsight of his experience is placed before the evidence of his blindness so that the irony of the situations in which he is placed may have full effect. The direct appeal of the Prologue for the audience to look into its own heart states openly what Wedekind's plays have consistently implied.

CONCLUSION

Wedekind's plays are set on the fringe of the respectable and bourgeois society from which the bulk of his audience, both in his lifetime and since, is drawn. Though the artist, the speculator and the confidence-trickster occupy the foreground of his works, Wedekind's real concern is to question the social morality that tolerates, and indeed spawns, such figures and to expose the rootless nature of the society in which his audience moves.

The smug complacency with which Wedekind's audiences watch him expose and ridicule the positions taken up by characters like Dr. Schön, Gerardo, the Marquis von Keith and King Nicolo is rudely shattered when the close similarity of the world on the stage and that of the audience is made clear. Much of the hostility that Wedekind aroused may reflect the general public's indignation at being made to wear a cap which they know fits all too well. Wedekind not only illustrates the faults in society, he refuses to let its members unload their complicity on to a scapegoat on the stage and requires his audience to live with the truth of the social conditions they have just seen in exaggerated form. This is the justification for art; it should make an audience think, and jolt it out of its complacency, but society depends on complacency and an acceptance of the *status quo* for its survival and is quick to forestall attempts to introduce change. This is the irony behind the terms in which Dr. Prantl objects to Buridan's writings in *Die Zensur*:

> We are not concerned about the effect your views have on *us*, our concern is for the unsuspecting member of the public who goes to one of your plays to relax and enjoy himself. He won't notice the moral harm you'll do him. (2; GW V, 123)

The crux of the matter is what is meant by 'moral harm'.

Wedekind's intention is to guide his audience and help them keep an open mind as to the relative motives of his characters. His use of scenic montage, of anticipation, variation and repetition in situation and character is extended and reflected in the register of vocabulary which his characters employ. There is a complex undercurrent of verbal implications in Wedekind's dialogue which it is impossible to render in translation because it is ingrained in the idiom and implications of the German language, but its effect is to tar all Wedekind's characters with the same brush. They may adopt different social masks, but they use the same terminology and unwittingly reveal the same fears and illusions.

The irony is that the characters on stage speak the language and think the thoughts that come naturally to the audience that is watching them. The 'unsuspecting member of the public' is thus presented with a caricature of his own situation which, Wedekind hopes, will cause him to reassess his position or at the least recognise it for a façade. It must be said, however, that the society to which Wedekind addressed himself in his lifetime had little to learn in the art of wilful myopia and deafness from the characters they saw, and today's audiences may conveniently hide behind the fiction that Wedekind's true significance is as an interesting eccentric in the history of theatre.

NOTES

1 Frank Wedekind, *Gesammelte Werke*, 9 vols., Munich, 1912–21. All quotations from Wedekind's work refer to this edition. (GW II, 126) indicates p. 126 of volume two. To assist readers using other editions, reference is also made to Act (II) and Scene (2). The full reference reads (II,2; GW II, 126): Where two quotations from the same scene follow in close proximity, the page reference only is given.

2 A. Kutscher, *Frank Wedekind. Sein Leben und Seine Werke*, 3 vols., Munich, 1922–31. This work was reissued in 1964 by List Verlag, Munich, in a much abridged edition by Karl Ude. Ude's version deletes much material useful to scholars but is still rather long for the more casual reader. A recent alternative introduction for the reader of German is Günter Seehaus's monograph in the Rowohlt series (see Bibliography).

3 Peter Barnes, *Lulu. A Sex Tragedy, Adapted from Wedekind's Earth Spirit and Pandora's Box*, London, 1971.
By convention, 'Lulu' is used to refer to the two Lulu plays where the reference is to the world in which Lulu moves rather than to a specific play. The convention is followed in this study.

4 W. Herzog, 'Frank Wedekind' in: *Menschen, denen ich begegnete*, Berne, 1959, p. 208.

5 Cf. Wedekind's published letter to Beate Heine, 11 February 1900.

6 K. Holm, *Farbiger Abglanz*, Munich, 1947, pp. 59–74.

7 Under the heading 'Die Weibsperson' (Female Person) in Wedekind's notebook (No. 34).

8 T. Durieux, *Eine Tür steht offen. Erinnerungen*, Berlin, 1954, p. 84.

9 J. Friedenthal (ed.), *Das Wedekindbuch*, Munich, 1914.

10 Tilly Wedekind, *Lulu, die Rolle meines Lebens*, Munich,

1969, p. 186. This fascinating autobiography throws much light on Wedekind as a person and offers valuable insights into the correlation between the author and his works.
11. *ibid.*, p. 188.
12. W. Sokel, *The Writer in Extremis. Expressionism in Twentieth Century German Literature*, Stanford, California, 1959, pp. 57–63.
13. F. Dürrenmatt, 'Theaterprobleme' in: *Theaterschriften und Reden*, Zurich, 1966, p. 124. Dürrenmatt's enthusiasm for Wedekind may be measured by a comparison between his play *Die Ehen des Herrn Mississippi* and Wedekind's *Schloss Wetterstein*. He wryly acknowledged his 'plagiarism' in: 'Bekenntnisse eines Plagiators', *Die Tat*, Zurich, 1952, No. 215.
14. F. Blei, 'Marginalien zu Wedekind' in: *Das Wedekindbuch*, p. 139.
15. In Wedekind's notebook (No. 58).
16. In Wedekind's notebook (No. 6) under the heading 'Der Witz' (The Joke).
17. L. R. Shaw's account in *The Playwright and Historical Change* (see bibliography) is recommended.
18. In *Was ich mir dabei dachte* (What I had in mind) (GW IX, 419–53). A collection of notes, thoughts and forewords to the plays.
19. *ibid.*
20. H. Maclean's articles on these plays (see bibliography) are recommended.
21. The 'Feenpalast' may well refer to Munich's 'Glaspalast' (Crystal Palace) which was at one time destined to become an experimental theatre for Richard Wagner. There are a number of 'coincidental' parallels. Those who are familiar with the play will recognise similarities in: Wilfrid Blunt, *The Dream King. Ludwig II of Bavaria*, Harmondsworth, 1973, pp. 33–45.
22. The earliest version of the play is a manuscript headed *Ein Genußmensch* (A Pleasure-seeker).

SELECT BIBLIOGRAPHY

I WORKS BY WEDEKIND

Frank Wedekind, *Gesammelte Werke*, 9 vols., Munich, 1912–21.
Frank Wedekind, *Ausgewählte Werke*, 5 vols., ed. Fritz Strich, Munich, 1924.

Recent collections of Wedekind's work:
Prosa, Dramen, Verse, 2 vols., selected by Hansgeorg Maier, Munich, 1954; 1964.
Werke, 3 vols., ed. with an intro. by Manfred Hahn, Aufbau, Berlin, 1969.
Stücke (Sonderausgabe), Nachwort von B. F. Sinnhuber, Langen-Müller, Munich, 1970.
(A fair range of texts is available in German paperbacks.)
Frank Wedekind, *Gesammelte Briefe*, 2 vols., ed. Fritz Strich, Munich, 1924.
Frank Wedekind, *Der vermummte Herr. Briefe Frank Wedekinds aus den Jahren 1881 bis 1917*, ed. W. Rasch, dtv 440, 1967. This contains 139 of the 479 letters of the 1924 edition.

II WEDEKIND IN ENGLISH TRANSLATION

A limited range of works has attracted enough interest to be translated. The list below is not exhaustive; where there are a number of translations of a play the most recent are shown. Many of the translations have dated very markedly and do Wedekind less than justice to a contemporary ear.

Collections
S. A. Eliot, Jr., *Tragedies of Sex*, New York, London, 1923. *(Spring's Awakening, Earth-Spirit, Pandora's Box, Damnation!)*. *Damnation!* is an alternative title to *Death and the Devil*.

F. Fawcett and S. Spender, *Five Tragedies of Sex*, London, 1952. (*Spring's Awakening, Earth Spirit, Pandora's Box, Death and the Devil*).

F. Fawcett and S. Spender, *Lulu and Other Sex Tragedies*, Calder and Boyars, London, 1973. (German Expressionism Series: The 1952 translations with the exception of *Spring's Awakening*.)

C. R. Mueller, *The Lulu Plays*, Greenwich, Conn., 1967. 'Newly translated and with an introduction by C. R. Mueller.' (*Earth Spirit, Pandora's Box, Death and the Devil*).

Death and the Devil is not, in fact, a Lulu play. It has one tenuous connection. A character called Casti-Piani, a procurer, appears in both *Pandora's Box* and *Death and the Devil*. He may or may not be the same person.

Individual Plays

Frühlings Erwachen

E. R. Bentley, *Spring's Awakening*, in: E. R. Bentley (ed.), *The Modern Theatre*, 6 vols., New York, 1955–60, vol. 6.

Tom Osborn, *Spring Awakening*, Calder and Boyars, London, 1969.

Das Sonnenspektrum (The Rainbow)

D. Faehl and E. Vaughn, *The Solar Spectrum; Those Who Buy the Gods of Love,* 'An Idyll from Modern Life', in: *Tulane Drama Review*, IV (1959), 108–38.

Der Kammersänger (The Court Singer)

A. Tridon, *The Tenor*, in: *Golden Book Magazine*, New York, V (1927), 65–73.

Translations by the same author in:

E. Hubermann and R. R. Raymo (eds.), *Angles of Vision*, Boston, 1962.

J. Gassner (ed.), *A Treasury of the Theatre*, revised edition, 3 vols., New York, Simon, 1963. vol. 2, *Modern European Drama*.

Lulu

Peter Barnes, *Lulu. A Sex Tragedy*, 'Adapted from Wedekind's *Earth Spirit* and *Pandora's Box*', Heinemann, London, 1971.

G. W. Pabst, *Pandora's Box, Classic Film Scripts* 29, translated from the German by Christopher Holme, Lorrimer Publishing, London, 1971.

Der Marquis von Keith

B. Gottlieb, *The Marquis of Keith*, in: E. R. Bentley (ed.), *From the Modern Repertoire*, Series Two, Indiana U.P., 1952.

and: H. M. Block and R. G. Shedd (eds.), *Masters of Modern Drama*, New York, 1962.

C. R. Mueller, *The Marquis of Keith*, in: R. W. Corrigan (ed.), *Masterpieces of The Modern German Theatre: Five Plays*, New York, 1967.

and: R. W. Corrigan (ed.), *The Modern Theatre*, New York, 1964.

König Nicolo

F. Ziegler, *Such is Life*, in: S. M. Tucker (ed.), *Modern Continental Plays*, New York, 1929;

and in: T. H. Dickinson (ed.), *Chief Contemporary Dramatists*, 3rd Series, Boston, 1930.

M. Esslin, *King Nicolo or Such is Life*, in: M. Esslin (ed.), *The Genius of the German Theater*, New York, 1968.

Recent Translations (as yet unpublished)

Edward Bond, *Spring Awakening*, for the National Theatre, London, May 1974.

Anthony Vivis, *The Marquis of Keith*, for B.B.C. Radio, February, 1972.

R. Eyre and A. Best, *The Marquis of Keith*, for the Royal Shakespeare Company, London, November 1974.

Secondary Works Consulted; a working bibliography

P. U. Beicken, 'Einige Bemerkungen zu Bergs *Lulu*', in: A. Goeze and G. P. Pflaum (eds.), *Vergleichen und verändern*, *Festschrift für Helmut Motekat*, Munich, 1970, pp. 196–207.

E. Bentley, *The Modern Theatre. A Study of Dramatists and the Drama*, London, 1948.

A. D. Best, 'The Censor Censored: An Approach to Frank Wedekind's *Die Zensur*', *German Life and Letters*, NS XXVI (1973), 278–87.

F. Blei, 'Marginalien zu Wedekind' in: J. Friedenthal (ed.), *Das Wedekindbuch*, Munich, 1914, pp. 128–50.

F. Blei, *Über Wedekind, Sternheim und das Theater*, Leipzig, 1915.

G. C. Boone, 'Zur inneren Entstehungsgeschichte von Wedekinds *Lulu*: eine neue These', *Etudes Germaniques*, XXVII (1972), 423–30.

K. Bullivant, 'The Notion of Morality in Wedekind's *Frühlings Erwachen*,' *New German Studies* (University of Hull), I (1973), 40–7.

B. Diebold, *Anarchie im Drama*, Frankfurt am Main, 1921.

T. Durieux, *Eine Tür steht offen. Erinnerungen*, Berlin, 1954.

F. Dürrenmatt, 'Bekenntnisse eines Plagiators', *Die Tat*, Zurich, 1952, No. 215.

F. Dürrenmatt, 'Theaterprobleme', in: F.D., *Theaterschriften und Reden*, ed. E. Brock-Sulzer, Zurich, 1966, pp. 92–131.

J. Elsom, *Erotic Theatre*, London, 1973, pp. 84–104.

W. Emrich, 'Die Lulu-Tragödie', in: B. von Wiese (ed.), *Das deutsche Drama vom Barock bis zur Gegenwart: Interpretationen*, 2 vols., Düsseldorf, 1958, vol. 2, pp. 207–28.

W. Emrich, 'Immanuel Kant und Frank Wedekind', in: W. E., *Polemik*, Frankfurt/Main, 1968, pp. 56–61.

R. Faesi, 'Frank Wedekind', in: H. Friedemann and Otto Mann (eds.), *Deutsche Literatur im 20. Jahrhundert. Strukturen und Gestalten*. 5 e. veränderte und erweiterte Auflage, ed. Otto Mann and W. Rothe, 2 vols., Berne/Munich, 1967, vol. 2, pp. 279–98.

P. Fechter, *Frank Wedekind. Der Mensch und das Werk*, Jena, 1920.

P. Fechter, *Das europäische Drama. Geist und Kultur im Spiegel des Theaters*, 3 vols., Mannheim, 1956–8, vol. 2.

L. Feuchtwanger, Introduction: Frances Fawcett and Stephen Spender, *Five Tragedies of Sex*, London, 1952.

R. A. Firda, 'Wedekind, Nietzsche and the Dionysian Experience', *Modern Language Notes*, LXXXVII (1972), 720–31.

J. Friedenthal (ed.), *Das Wedekindbuch*, Munich, 1914.

H. F. Garten, *Modern German Drama*, London, 1959.

S. Gittleman, 'Frank Wedekind's Image of America', *German Quarterly*, XXXIV (1966), 570–80.

S. Gittleman, 'Frank Wedekind and Bertolt Brecht: Notes on a Relationship', *Modern Drama*, X (1967), 401–09.

S. Gittleman, *Frank Wedekind* (Twayne World Authors Series), New York, 1969.

M. Gravier, 'Strindberg et Wedekind', *Etudes Germaniques*, III (1948), 309–18.

F. Gundolf, 'Frank Wedekind', *Trivium*, Zurich, VI (1948),

187–217. (Republished by Langen-Müller, Munich, 1954 as: Langen-Müllers kleine Geschenkbücher, No. 25.)

H. Günther, 'Paris als Erlebnis, Frank Wedekind in Paris', *Antares*, I (1952–3), 3–8.

W. Hartwig, 'Materialien zur Interpretation', Frank Wedekind, *Der Marquis von Keith*, Komedia, No. 8, Berlin, 1965.

W. Herzog, *Menschen, denen ich begegnete*, Berne, 1959.

F. W. J. Heuser, 'Gerhart Hauptmann and Frank Wedekind', *Germanic Review*, XX (1945), 54–68. (Republished in German, in: F.W.J.H., *Gerhart Hauptmann. Zu seinem Leben und Schaffen*, Tübingen, 1961.)

C. Hill, 'Wedekind in Retrospect', *Modern Drama*, III (1960–1), 82–92.

K. Holm, *Farbiger Abglanz*, Munich, 1947.

R. A. Jones, 'Frank Wedekind: Circus Fan', *Monatshefte*, LXI (1969), 139–56.

H. Kaufmann, 'Zwei Dramatiker: Gerhart Hauptmann und Frank Wedekind', in: H.K., *Krisen und Wandlungen der deutschen Literatur von Wedekind bis Feuchtwanger*, Aufbau, Berlin, 1966, 45–81.

K. Kraus, 'Die Büchse der Pandora', in: K.K., *Literatur und Lüge*, Munich 1958, 9–21. (=vol. 6 of Kraus' collected works). Originally published in *Die Fackel*, May 1905.

P. G. Krohn, 'Frank Wedekinds politische Gedichte', *Neue deutsche Literatur*, VI (1958), 84–95.

A. Kutscher, *Frank Wedekind. Sein Leben und seine Werke*, 3 vols., Munich, 1922–31. (Reissued in one abridged volume, ed. Karl Ude, List, Munich, 1964.)

A. Kutscher, 'Wedekind und der Zirkus', *Faust*, Berlin, III (1924), 1–5.

A. Kutscher, 'Eine unbekannte französische Quelle zu Wedekinds *Erdgeist* und *Büchse der Pandora*', *Das goldene Tor*, Baden-Baden, II (1947), 497–505.

H. Maclean, 'Expressionism', in: J. M. Ritchie (ed.), *Periods in German Literature*, London, 1966, pp. 257–80.

H. Maclean, 'Wedekind's *Der Marquis von Keith*: An Interpretation based on the Faust and Circus Motifs', *Germanic Review*, XLIII (1968), 163–87.

H. Maclean, 'The King and the Fool in Wedekind's *König Nicolo*', *Seminar*, V (1969), 21–35.

H. Maclean, 'Polarity and Synthesis of the Sexes in Frank Wedekind's Work', *AULLA*, XIII (1970), 231–42.

M. Maclean, 'Jean Giraudoux and Frank Wedekind', *AJFS*, IV (1967), 97–105.

T. Mann, 'Über eine Szene von Wedekind', in: J. Friedenthal (ed.), *Das Wedekindbuch*, (s.a.) pp. 215–24. Also in: T.M., *Gesammelte Werke in 12 Bänden*, Fischer, 1960, vol. 10, *Reden and Aufsätze*, pp. 70–6.

P. Michelsen, 'Frank Wedekind' in: B. von Wiese (ed.), *Deutsche Dichter der Moderne*, Berlin, 1965, pp. 49–67.

D. Mitchell, 'The Character of Lulu: Wedekind's and Berg's Conceptions Compared', *Music Review*, XV (1954), 268–74.

A. Natan, 'Frank Wedekind' in: A. Natan (ed.), *German Men of Letters*, vol. 2, London, 1963, 103–29.

E. S. Neumann, 'Musik in Frank Wedekinds Bühnenwerken', *German Quarterly*, XLIV (1971), 35–47.

C. Quigier, 'L'érotisme de Frank Wedekind', *Etudes Germaniques*, XVII (1962), 14–33.

W. Rasch, 'Sozialkritische Aspekte in Wedekinds dramatischer Dichtung. Sexualität, Kunst und Gesellschaft', in: W.R., *Gestaltungsgeschichte und Gesellschaftsgeschichte*, Stuttgart, 1969, pp. 409–26.

F. Rothe, *Frank Wedekinds Dramen. Jugendstil und Philosophie*, Stuttgart, 1968.

F. Rothe, '*Frühlings Erwachen*. Zum Verhältnis von sexueller und sozialer Emanzipation bei Frank Wedekind', *Studi Germanici*, VII (1969), 30–41.

R. Samuel and R. Hinton-Thomas, *Expressionism in German Life, Literature and Theatre (1910–24)*, Cambridge, 1939.

G. Seehaus, *Frank Wedekind und das Theater*, Munich, 1964.

G. Seehaus, *Frank Wedekind* (Rowohlts Monographien Nr. 213), Hamburg, 1974.

O. Seidlin, 'Frank Wedekind's German-American Parents', *American-German Review*, XII (1946), 24–6.

L. R. Shaw, 'Bekenntnis und Erkenntnis in Wedekind's *Die Zensur*', in: R. Lemp (ed.), *Frank Wedekind zum 100. Geburtstag*, Munich, 1964, pp. 20–36.

L. R. Shaw, 'The Strategy of Reformulation: *Frühlings Erwachen*', in: L.R.S., *The Playwright and Historical Change. Dramatic Strategies in Brecht, Hauptmann, Kaiser and Wedekind*, University of Wisconsin Press, 1970, pp. 49–65.

- W. Sokel, *The Writer in Extremis. Expressionism in Twentieth Century German Literature*, Stanford, California, 1959, pp. 57–63.
- W. Sokel, 'The Changing Role of Eros in Wedekind's Drama', *German Quarterly*, XXXIX (1966), 201–7.
- F. Strich, 'Frank Wedekind', in F.S., *Dichtung und Zivilisation*, Munich, 1928. (This first appeared as the Introduction to Frank Wedekind, *Ausgewählte Werke*. See above.)
- K. Völker, *Frank Wedekind* (Friedrichs Dramatiker des Welttheaters, 7), Hanover, 1965.
- G. Weales, 'The Slippery Business of Frank Wedekind', *American-German Review*, XXXIV (1967–8), 41–44.
- K. Wedekind-Biel, 'A Scene from an Unpublished Version of Frank Wedekind's Lulu Tragedy', *Modern Drama*, IV (1961–2), 97–100.
- P. Wedekind, Introduction: Frank Wedekind, *Der Kammersänger*, (Reclam) Stuttgart, 1959.
- T. Wedekind, *Lulu, die Rolle meines Lebens*, Munich, 1969.
- A. D. White, 'The Notion of Morality in Wedekind's *Frühlings Erwachen*: A Comment', *New German Studies*, I (1973), 116–18 (cf. under Bullivant above).